AF541083

FLIGHT CONTROL
Geometric Algorithms

FLIGHT CONTROL
Geometric Algorithms

MICHAEL MOORE

KNOWLEDGE BAKERS

Cataloging in Publication Data--DK

Courtesy: D.K. Agencies (P) Ltd. <docinfo@dkagencies.com>

Moore, Michael (Writer on flight control), **author.**

Flight control : geometric algorithms / by Michael Moore.

pages cm

Includes bibliographical references.

ISBN 9789391502591

1. Flight control. I. Title.

LCC TL589.4.M66 2023 | DDC 629.1326 23

ISBN: 978-93-91502-59-1

Published by : **Knowledge Bakers**
Pune, India
Email: knowledgebakers2019@gmail.com

Digitally Printed at : **Replika Press Pvt. Ltd.**

ACKNOWLEDGMENTS

I would like to take this opportunity to thank my first supervisor Prof. Mikhail Goman and second supervisor Prof. Gwynne Evans for the support and encouragement which they gave me during my work. I express my sincerest gratitude to them for carefully reading and correcting parts of this manuscript.

I am also thankful to my internal examiner Prof. Bogumil Ulanicki and external one Dr. Alexandros Smerlas, who was at the time working at Eurocopter Germany GmbH as Research and Development Engineer, for their constructive suggestions, which have helped me to improve the quality of the thesis.

I want also to express my thanks to Mr. Grahame Hudson and Ms. Charlotte Kitson from the International Research Office for their tremendous support of the collaborative programme between DMU and Russian universities. I am indebted to the Director of Software Technology Research Laboratory (STRL) Prof. Hussein Zedan, who sheltered me there and provided an excellent academic environment.

I deeply appreciate also the financial support provided by the University during my studies. It came from many different sources, including travel grants for visiting DMU in the beginning of my PhD programme, and part-time jobs that I've done for STRL under the supervision of Prof. Zedan and for Emerging Technologies Research Centre under the supervision of Dr. Merlyne Maria De Souza. The final preparation of this thesis would be nearly impossible without help from Pro-Vice Chancellor Prof. Jeffrey Knight, who authorized my full-time studies at DMU during the last four years.

Finally I pay tribute to my Russian Alma Mater, the Faculty of Informatics and Control Systems at the Bauman Moscow State Technical University and my supervisor there Dr. Nikolay Filimonov, who did open me the way to the world of Control Systems.

Michael Moore

CONTENTS

LIST OF FIGURES

LIST OF TABLES

Page

Chapter 1

Introduction

In nature, unstable things are often more efficient than stable things.

Jerrold Marsden

In this thesis novel numerical algorithms are developed to solve some problems of analysis and control design for input constrained linear dynamical systems. Although the results obtained are of a general nature, all the problems considered are induced by flight control applications. The thesis therefore should be considered as a combination of two subjects, namely, Electronic and Electrical Engineering from which it borrows control theory and methods, and Aerospace Engineering from which it borrows motivation and application examples.

All the problems considered here are stated in terms of geometry, and because of this their solutions in the thesis were effectively achieved by geometrically-oriented methods. More specifically, during the solution of the problems mentioned above we consider modern geometric optimality criteria. We either maximize the size of some set in Euclidean n-dimensional space, or we have to somehow estimate its size. Considering these optimality criteria, we apply some operations on sets, e.g. boundary points search, to solve the problem and arrive at some computational algorithm.

For validation of the algorithms developed, we perform simulation of the closed-loop system on a grid of state-space points, investigating linearized models of flight vehicles or their parts.

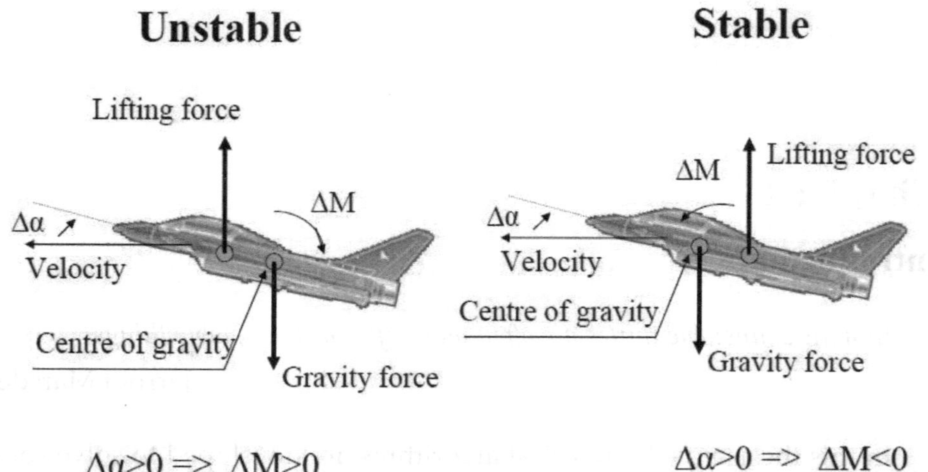

Figure 1.1: Stable and unstable configurations of an aircraft. Here $\Delta\alpha$ - the angle of attack and ΔM - the pitching moment around centre of gravity.

Let us now briefly describe problems in flight control that serve as a motivation for this thesis and their connection with the corresponding problems in general control theory, which we address in the following chapters.

1.1 Controllable region assessment

An aerodynamically unstable aircraft configuration stabilized by a control system has a potential to overcome many conventional design limitations. For example, such an aircraft configuration can possess a higher lift to drag ratio, the critical flight regimes such as high incidence departures or aeroelastic instabilities can be significantly relaxed or even eliminated by implementation of a control system. Hence, the active control approach to air vehicle design grants the opportunity for improvement of air vehicle dynamic and performance characteristics.

At flight regimes with dynamic instability (see Fig. 1.1), aircraft motion can be locally represented by a linear time invariant system with exponentially unstable eigenvalues. In this case an important problem in the design of the control laws is connected with a realistic account of actuator constraints such as deflection limits and rate saturation.

The unstable linear system with constrained control inputs has a bounded *controllable region*, which is a set of system states that can be stabilized by any realizable control action (i.e. under amplitude and rate constraints).

This means that the stabilization problem under the restriction of a control input can be solved only for a limited set of initial states of the system.

Consider as an example the following one-dimensional system:

$$\dot{x} = x + u, \; |u| \leq 1.$$

The stability criterion for $x > 0$ is of the form $\dot{x} < 0$, which means $x < -u$. Therefore, any initial state $x_0 > 1$ (as well as $x_0 < -1$) cannot be driven to the origin.

The size of the controllable region for the open-loop unstable system with constrained control inputs can serve as a controllability measure for the control design problem. If external disturbances move the system outside the controllable region, nothing is able to keep the system stable.

1.2 Stability region design

The *stability region* (or *domain of attraction*) for the closed-loop system by definition is the set of states that are stabilizable by a particular controller. The stability region generally utilizes only a part of the open-loop system controllable region and cannot exceed it. In some cases a "good" controller in terms of linear system criteria such as local stability and robust performance can provide the closed-loop system with a very small and unsatisfactory stability region, given the limitations imposed by actuator constraints (Hanson and Stengel, 1984; Shrivastava and Stengel, 1989). Therefore, an additional design objective may be formulated as maximizing the region of attraction for the closed-loop system. This objective maximizes the level of external disturbances, from which the nominal mode of system operation can be restored after they are cancelled.

Different controllers in the closed-loop system produce stability regions having different sizes, which never exceed the size of the corresponding controllable region. So, the ratio between a stability-controllable region pair can be attributed to the controller as its performance measure and considered as a characteristic complementing its other linear properties (see Fig. 1.2). This new measure has been proposed in (Goman, Fedulova and Khramtsovsky, 1996).

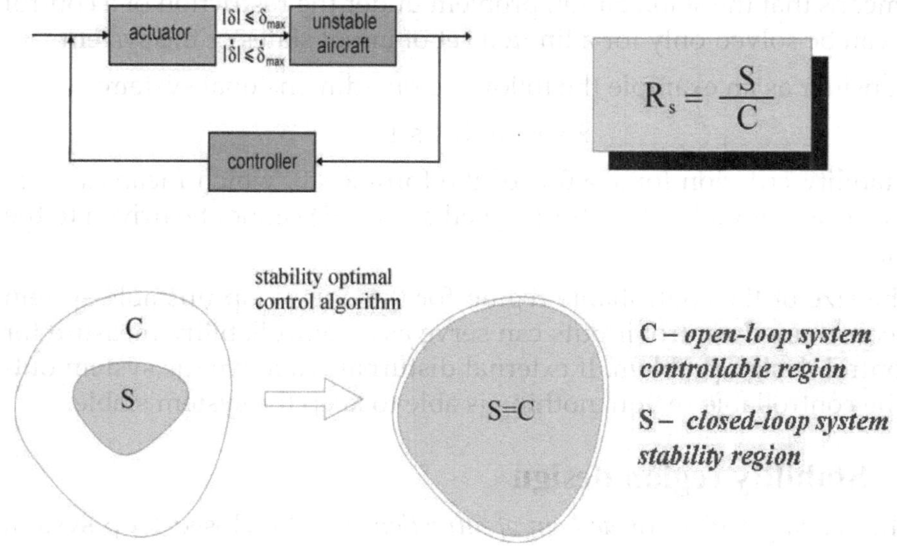

Figure 1.2: Set-based performance measure

1.3 Comparison of the regions

The direct comparison of multidimensional stability and controllable regions can be replaced by consideration of their two-dimensional cross-sections or *slices*. Different combinations of two-dimensional cross-sections help to visualize multidimensional regions and significantly simplifies the comparative analysis due to relatively small computational demands.

Consider as an example the following linear system having two complex eigenvalues:

$$A = \begin{bmatrix} 0 & 1 \\ -2.1 & 1.91 \end{bmatrix}, B = \begin{bmatrix} 0.1 & 0 \\ 0 & 0.1 \end{bmatrix}, \begin{bmatrix} -20 \\ -20 \end{bmatrix} \leq u \leq \begin{bmatrix} 20 \\ 20 \end{bmatrix}.$$

Let consider a regulator designed via pole placement technique:

$$u = Kx, \text{ where } K = \begin{bmatrix} -9.55 & -20.9 \\ 31.9 & -28.6 \end{bmatrix}.$$

This regulator provides the closed-loop system with the following poles: $-0.9525 \pm 1.09j$. In Fig. 1.3 stability region (solid) is shown in comparison with the controllable one. This region is clearly nonconvex, and its computation was made via numerical integration. The dotted curves represent trajectories of the closed-loop system.

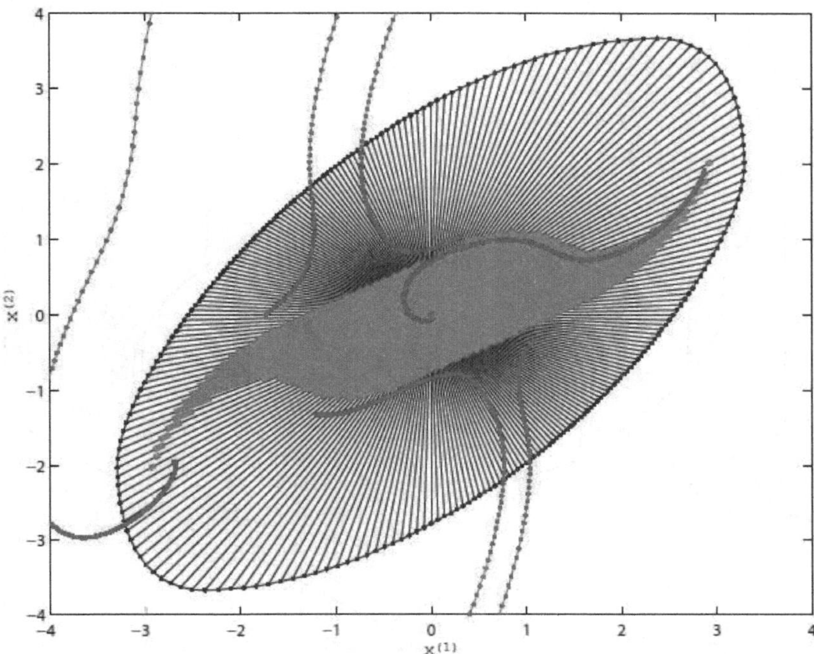

Figure 1.3: An example of two-dimensional system with two controls: a graphical comparison between the stability and the controllable regions.

However, it should be emphasized that this comparison gives us only necessary, but not sufficient conditions for controller assessment. The closeness of some cross-sections of stability and controllable regions does not guarantee their closeness in differently oriented cross-sections in multidimensional state space. Nevertheless, the proposed method provides the possibility for identification of unacceptable controllers.

In this thesis the computation of two-dimensional slices of the stability region is performed by direct numerical simulation of the closed-loop system on a fine grid of points located in two-dimensional plane. Then the slice of stability region or region of attraction is defined precisely by those points, for which trajectories started from them tend to the origin.

Similar computation of controllable region on a grid of points is much more time consuming as it requires to solve a two-boundary value problem for each grid point. Fortunately, the controllable region for systems under consideration is convex and it can be restored by computation of its boundary points.

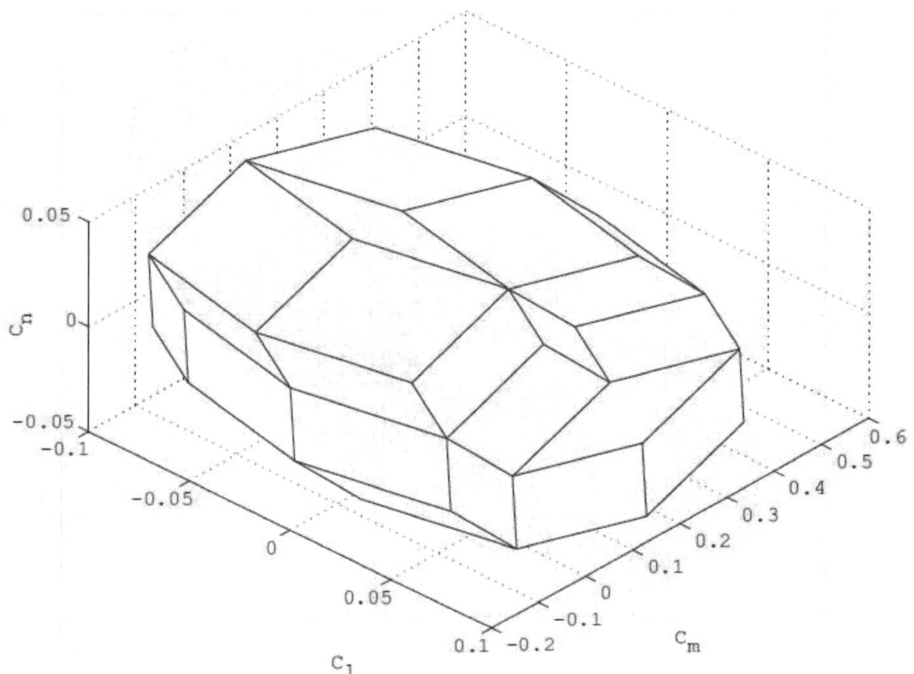

Figure 1.4: An example of attainable moment set for the F-18 fighter aircraft

1.4 Control allocation problem

When an aircraft has multiple control effectors producing forces and moments along different axes, the control allocation problem may not be unique. The required forces and moments to solve the control problem can be distributed between control effectors in different ways and therefore some additional criteria are required to perform such allocation.

A typical modern manoeuvrable aircraft has a redundant number of aerodynamic surfaces, such as left and right stabilators, ailerons, rudder, left and right leading flaps, left and right canard surfaces. In addition, some aircraft (e.g. Su-30, F/A-18 HARV, X-31) are equipped with the thrust vectoring control generating significant control moments at low speed and high incidence flight, which much exceed the aerodynamic control margins under these flight conditions. The advanced aircraft configurations will possess an even greater number of control effectors.

The aircraft flight control and angular stabilization require some definite margins both in force and moment control powers to maintain the flight, provide the agility and to reject possible external disturbances. So, the assessment of the extreme control capabilities for specific flight conditions and type of maneuvering is an important problem at the prelimi-nary stage of an aircraft design.

This problem can be formulated without considering the aircraft dynamic equations and time consuming mathematical simulations.

Every manoeuvre needs application of some definite magnitudes of forces and moments and some additional control margins should be available for disturbance rejection. To meet all design specifications for aircraft configuration and control system the knowledge about the attainable moment set is important. The attainable set of points for moment control (see Fig. 1.4) can be a good relative measure of different aircraft configurations with redundant control effectors.

Note, that the control allocation procedure can be performed in different ways depending on the performance objectives and any algorithm can only reduce the size of the attainable moment set. Mathematically, the procedure corresponds to a real-time solution of the classical root finding problem for a system of overdetermined equations. In the same way as for controllable and stability regions, the relation between sizes of the actual and the attainable moment set for the given control allocation algorithm can be a good metric for its assessment.

The problem of choosing a control allocation technique can be considered also from the viewpoint of the stability region size, and in this context it is also a logical continuation of the previous two problems considered in the thesis. It is well recognized that a control allocation algorithm may affect the closed-loop behaviour (Buffington and Enns, 1996). The stability region measure might be useful in comparison between different allocation methods. It is expected that the methods, which yield maximum possible control allocation (Durham, 1994; Petersen and Bodson, 2000), also provide maximum achievable stability region while preserving the same controller in the closed-loop system.

1.5 Summary of contents

Each Chapter of this thesis represents some particular analysis or design problem, and has its own bibliography review and a specific set of numerical examples. The contents are briefly outlined below.

In *Chapters 2 and 3* the analysis and design problems that are specific for unstable linear time-invariant systems are considered.

Chapter 2 is connected with the analysis of the controllable region. In Sections 2.1, 2.2 literature review of the previous development in the field is provided with the emphasis on polyhedral methods for controllable regions computation. In Section 2.3 the notion of controllable region slices is introduced, and it is shown how we can use them to compare stability and controllable regions. In Section 2.4 a numerical algorithm for the computation of two-dimensional slices of the region is proposed, which is based on a numerically robust solution of two-boundary value problems for unstable linear systems.

In *Chapter 3* we consider the problem of stabilizing exponentially unstable linear systems with saturating actuators. For systems having up to two exponentially unstable open-loop poles and multiple control inputs, we provide a geometric insight into how to construct a saturated stabilizing linear state feedback so that to maximize a domain of attraction of a closed-loop system. In Section 3.3 a controller which is optimal in this sense is proposed for the case of one unstable eigenvalue and many control inputs. In Section 3.4 this development is enhanced to cover the case of two unstable eigenvalues.

In *Chapter 4* a linear control allocation problem is considered for overactuated systems and its real-time solution is suggested. To address this problem, polytopic representation of an attainable set is considered in Section 4.3 and its properties are discussed. In Section 4.4 an algorithm based on the notion of generalized bisection is derived for systems of linear overdetermined equations with constrained variables.

Alongside with theoretical descriptions, the proposed algorithms are validated in each chapter using linearized mathematical models arising from flight dynamics.

1.6 Original results and their dissemination

This thesis is based on open sources of information and no material used here was classified by commercial or any other reasons. All original contributions of the thesis, listed below, have been published in refereed conference proceedings, a journal and a book before its final submission.

- A numerical algorithm for the computation of two-dimensional slices of the controllable region. The dynamical systems considered are linear with interval amplitude and rate control constraints. The preliminary version of this algorithm was presented at the AIAA Navigation, Guidance and Control Conference (Goman and Demenkov, 2002). The final version, which is described in Chapter 2, has been published in the AIAA Journal of Guidance, Control and Dynamics (Goman and Demenkov, 2004*a*).

- A stability optimal controller for the case of one and two exponentially unstable eigen-values and many control inputs. The dynamical systems considered are linear with amplitude control constraints. The first version of the algorithm has been published as an invited book chapter (Goman and Demenkov, 2004*b*). The second version, which makes use of the LMI formulation, was presented at the UKACC International Control Conference (Demenkov, 2006). Both versions constitute Chapter 3.
- A control allocation algorithm that yields the solution in a finite number of iterations, while utilizing whole attainable set of solutions. The systems of equations considered are linear two-or three-dimensional with interval-constrained variables. The preliminary version of the algorithm has been published in the AIAA Navigation, Guidance and Control Conference proceedings (Demenkov, 2005), although it was not actually presented there. The final version, which is described in Chapter 4, was presented at the 17th IFAC Symposium on Automatic Control in Aerospace (Demenkov, 2007).

The contents of the thesis are the results of the original research unless otherwise stated and have not been submitted for a higher degree at any other university or institution. The material described in the thesis has been obtained under the supervision of Prof. Mikhail Goman. Some application results have been obtained in cooperation with him. However, the majority of the work (approximately 90%) is done by the author.

1.7 Notations and abbreviations

Vectors are supposed to be column if the opposite is not stated.

I	identity matrix
Rn	n-dimensional Euclidean space
$R^{n\times m}$	$n \times m$ real matrix
x^T	transposed vector
$[x;y]$	$[x^T\ y^T]^T$
(x, y)	two-dimensional plane spanned by vectors x and y
$0_{m\times n}$	$m \times n$ matrix of zeros
$x^{(i)}$	the i-th component of vector x
x_{min}	vector of minimum limits for components of the vector x

x_{max}	vector of maximum limits for components of the vector x
$\|\|x\|\|_2$	2-norm: $\sqrt{x^{T}x}$
$\|\|x\|\|_\infty$	infinity-norm: $\max_{i=\overline{1,n}} \|x^{(i)}\|$
x_i	the i-th column of a matrix or the i-th vector in a sequence
$[x, y, ...]$	row vector with components $x, y, ...$
$t \in [t_1, t_2]$	t belongs to an interval between t_1 and t_2
$Re\ \lambda$	real part of the complex number λ
$\in, \subseteq$	belongs to
$\forall$	for all
$i = \overline{1,n}$	$i = 1, 2, ..., n$
$\{x,\ y,\ ...\}, \{x_i\}_{i=\overline{1,n}}$	set of vectors $x, y, ...$ or $x_1, x_2, ...$
1D	one-dimensional
2D	two-dimensional
3D	three-dimensional
LQ, LQR	linear-quadratic regulator
LP, QP	linear and quadratic programming
FME	Fourier-Motzkin elimination
LMI	linear matrix inequalities
APS	attainable pseudocontrol set

Chapter 2

Computation of Controllable Regions

In this chapter an algorithm based on a convex optimization technique is proposed for computation of the controllable region of an unstable linear system under amplitude and rate control constraints.

In the first part of this chapter, a review of known methods of controllable region analysis is given. The second part contains a description of the proposed computational algorithm, which is based on the solution of a linear programming problem. In the third part examples of the controllable region analysis for an aeroservoelastic airfoil system and to a reusable launch vehicle are presented to illustrate the capabilities of the proposed algorithm.

2.1 Some theoretical properties of controllable region

Let us consider the following open-loop unstable continuous-time system:

$$\dot{x}(t) = Ax(t) + Bu(t), \tag{2.1}$$

where $A \in R^{n\times n}$ has eigenvalues with positive real parts, $B \in R^{n\times m}$, $x \in R^n$ and $u \in U$. Here $U \in R^m$ is a compact (i.e. overall bounded) set. It is additionally supposed that the state vector x is fully observable and $n > 1$.

All eigenvalues λ_i, $i = 1, ..., n$ of matrix A in (2.1) can be divided into stable ($Re\,\lambda_i < 0$), neutral ($Re\,\lambda_i = 0$) and unstable (also called anti-stable) ($Re\,\lambda_i > 0$) groups. Here $Re\,\lambda_i$ is the real part of λ_i.

While the stability of an equilibrium in a linear system is a global property, the stability of an equilibrium in a nonlinear system is just a local characteristic. The unstable linear system in (2.1) under any control law with constrained inputs becomes nonlinear and can be stable only in a bounded region of the state-space, known as *stability region* or *region of attraction*. The maximum attainable region of attraction coincides with the *controllable region*, which is also called the *asymptotically null controllable region* (Formalsky, 1968; Goman et al., 1996; Hu and Lin, 2001*b*). Theoretical investigation of controllable region boundedness has been done in (Ma, 1991; Lee and Hedrick, 1995; Zhao and Jayasariya, 1995).

Note that a control function $u(t)$ that satisfies only deflection constraints can be discontinuous. The controllable and stability regions in this case can be specified only in the system state-space, because the reachability of the origin from any initial state does not depend on initial values of control vector. In some cases a control function $u(t)$ steering an initial state from the controllable region to the origin can be of the bang-bang type (Hu and Lin, 2001*b*; Formalsky, 1968), i.e. piecewise-constant and discontinuous. The possibility of discontinuous control significantly simplifies the computation of the controllable region.

Rate constraints, imposed on control inputs, preserve continuity of the control function. In this case the reachability of the origin from some initial states of the system depends on the initial positions of actuators. This means that the controllable region of the open-loop system and the stability region for the closed-loop system must be defined in the extended state+control space.

We will first give some theoretical results for the region of first kind, i.e. considering amplitude constraints only.

Definition 1 *The controllable region C of the system (2.1) is the set of all points $x \in R^n$ such that for each initial condition $x(0) = x$ the control function $u(t) \in U$ exists and the solution of the controlled system asymptotically tends to origin:*

$$C = \{x \in R^n : x(0) = x, u(t) \in U, \forall i = \overline{1,n} \lim_{t\to\infty} x^{(i)}(t) = 0\}.$$

It can be easily shown that the controllable region is convex.

Theorem 1 *The controllable region C is convex if U is convex.*

Proof: The solution of linear differential equation (2.1) has the form:

$$x(t) = e^{At}x(0) + \int_0^t e^{A(t-\tau)}Bu(\tau)d\tau,$$

where e^{At} is the matrix exponential.

Suppose that the controllable region is not convex. In this case there always exist two points $x_1(0) \in C$ and $x_2(0) \in C$ such that at least one point $x_3(0) \notin C$ exists, where $x_3(0)$ is taken from a line segment generated by these points. Since $x_1(0) \in C$, $x_2(0) \in C$ control functions $u_1(t) \in U$, $u_2(t) \in U$

exist such that $x_1(t) \to 0$, $x_2(t) \to 0$ as $t \to \infty$.

Let us write $x_3(0)$ as a convex combination of $x_1(0)$ and $x_2(0)$:

$$x_3(0) = \lambda_1 x_1(0) + \lambda_2 x_2(0),\ \lambda_1 + \lambda_2 = 1,\ \lambda_1 \geq 0,\ \lambda_2 \geq 0.$$

Take the control function $u_3(t)$ as follows:

$$u_3(t) = \lambda_1 u_1(t) + \lambda_2 u_2(t).$$

Note that $u_3(t)$ belongs to a line segment generated by $u_1(t) \in U$ and $u_2(t) \in U$ and therefore $u_3(t) \in U$ if U is convex.

Now, it is easy to show that the solution $x_3(t)$ from an initial state $x_3(0)$ is the convex combination of solutions $x_1(t)$ and $x_2(t)$:

$$x_3(t) = e^{At}(\lambda_1 x_1(0) + \lambda_2 x_2(0)) + \int_0^t e^{A(t-\tau)} B(\lambda_1 u_1(t) + \lambda_2 u_2(t)) d\tau = \lambda_1 x_1(t) + \lambda_2 x_2(t).$$

From the convergence of $x_1(t)$, $x_2(t)$ to the origin we have:

$$\lim_{t\to\infty} x_3^{(i)}(t) = \lim_{t\to\infty} (\lambda_1 x_1^{(i)}(t) + \lambda_2 x_2^{(i)}(t)) = \lambda_1 \lim_{t\to\infty} x_1^{(i)}(t) + \lambda_2 \lim_{t\to\infty} x_2^{(i)}(t) = 0,$$

that is, $x_3(0) \in C$ and this is contrary to our assumption of non-convexity of C.

To reduce the dimension in the analysis and synthesis tasks, it is natural to take into account only the subspace corresponding to the unstable and neutral eigenvalues, with the possible inclusion of some stable eigenvalues which are in the neighbourhood of the stability boundary. There are two popular state transformations that we can use for this purpose: the first one is based on the Schur decomposition (Castelan, da Silva Jr. and Cury, 1996; Golub and Loan, 1986) of the system matrix A and the second one is based on the block Jordan decomposition of the matrix A. We restrict our attention on the Schur decomposition as the most robust and reliable, even in the case of multiple and defective eigenvalues.

Let us suppose that n system matrix eigenvalues are arranged in a list in increasing order of its real part with the first $n-q$ desirable stable eigenvalues and the last q undesirable ones (for example neutral, unstable and stable but with low degree of stability). The stable and neutral eigenvalues are placed in the beginning of the undesirable part of the list. Consider the following transformation of basis in (2.1):

$$x = [Q_1 \mid Q_2] \begin{bmatrix} s \\ z \end{bmatrix}$$

where the matrix $Q = [Q_1 | Q_2]$ is orthogonal ($Q^T Q = I$) and such that the columns of $Q_1 \in R^{n\times(n-q)}$ and $Q_2 \in R^{n\times q}$ span the subspaces associated with the desirable and undesirable eigenvalues, correspondingly. This matrix can be obtained from a Schur decomposition of matrix A by reordering, if necessary, eigenvalues of its diagonal blocks (Golub and Loan, 1986) in accordance with the eigenvalue list formed.

In the new basis the open-loop system is represented by

$$\begin{bmatrix} \dot{s}(t) \\ \dot{z}(t) \end{bmatrix} = Q^T A Q \begin{bmatrix} s(t) \\ z(t) \end{bmatrix} + Q^T B u(t) = \begin{bmatrix} A_{11} & A_{12} \\ 0 & A_z \end{bmatrix} \begin{bmatrix} s(t) \\ z(t) \end{bmatrix} + \begin{bmatrix} B_1 \\ B_z \end{bmatrix} u(t)$$

where the eigenvalues of matrices A_{11} and A_z contain the desirable and undesirable ones, correspondingly.

Note, that the dynamics of $z(t)$ associated with the undesirable eigenvalues is decoupled from $s(t)$. Thus we can isolate the following open-loop reduced-order system:

$$\dot{z}(t) = A_z z(t) + B_z u(t), \tag{2.2}$$

where $A_z \in R^{q\times q}$, $B_z \in R^{q\times m}$ and $z(t) = Q_2^T x(t)$. If the state of system (2.2) is kept in its equilibrium point with $z(t) = 0$ and $u(t) = 0$, it is trivial to show that $s(t)$ asymptotically tends to the origin and thus we need to stabilize only system (2.2).

The following very important property explains, why one cannot stabilize the unstable system using bounded controls in the whole state-space.

Theorem 2 *Suppose that our linear system has only anti-stable eigenvalues and control vector that is constrained. Then the controllable region C of the system is a bounded set:*

$$\sup_{x\in C} ||x||_2 < \infty.$$

Proof: The solution of linear differential equation (2.1) has the form:

$$x(t) = e^{At}x(0) + \int_0^t e^{A(t-\tau)} Bu(\tau)d\tau,$$

and from this equation with $x(t) = 0$ and $t \to \infty$ we have:

$$x(0) = -\int_0^\infty e^{-A\tau} Bu(\tau)d\tau = -\sum_{i=1}^m x_i, \quad x_i = \int_0^\infty e^{-A\tau} b_i u^{(i)}(\tau)d\tau.$$

The last equation describes all the points $x(0) \in C$.

Now we have to prove that for any control function $u(\tau)$, $||x(0)||_2 < \infty$. Clearly,

$$||x(0)||_2 \leq \sum_{i=1}^{m} ||x_i||_2,$$

and it is enough to prove inequality $||x_i||_2 < \infty$.

Note that for the vector 2-norm the matrix 2-norm is defined for a matrix $M \in C^{n\times n}$ as (Golub and Loan, 1986):

$$||M||_2 = \sup_{x\neq 0} \frac{||Mx||_2}{||x||_2},$$

and $||M||_2||x||_2 \leq ||Mx||_2$.

$$\begin{aligned} ||x_i||_2 &= ||\int_0^\infty e^{-A\tau} b_i u^{(i)}(\tau) d\tau||_2 \leq \int_0^\infty ||e^{-A\tau} b_i u^{(i)}(\tau)||_2 d\tau \leq \int_0^\infty ||e^{-A\tau}||_2 ||b_i u^{(i)}(\tau)||_2 d\tau \\ &\leq ||b_i u^{(i)}_{max}||_2 \int_0^\infty ||e^{-A\tau}||_2 d\tau. \end{aligned}$$

Let us recall the following inequality (Golub and Loan, 1986) for a matrix $A \in R^{n\times n}$:

$$||e^{A\tau}||_2 \leq e^{\alpha\tau M_s(\tau)},$$

where $\alpha = \max\limits_{1\leq i\leq n} \{Re\ \lambda_i : \lambda_i \in \lambda(A)\}$ (here $\lambda(A) = \{\lambda_1, ..., \lambda_n\}$ is the set of all eigenvalues of A) and

$$M_s(\tau) = \sum_{k=0}^{n-1} \frac{||N\tau||_2^k}{k!},$$

here $k! = 1$ if $k = 0$. The matrix N in the above equation is computed from complex Schur decomposition of matrix A:

$$Q^T AQ = D + N,$$

where $Q \in R^{n\times n}$, $Q^T Q = I$, $D = diag(\lambda_1, ..., \lambda_n) \in R^{n\times n}$ is the diagonal matrix with eigenvalues of A on its diagonal and zeros in all other elements, and $N \in R^{n\times n}$ is the upper triangular matrix.

Now we have to prove that $\int_0^\infty ||e^{-A\tau}||_2 d\tau < \infty$.

For an anti-stable matrix A, all eigenvalues of $-A$ are stable and $\alpha < 0$. For $n = 1$, $Ms(\tau) = 1$ and

$$\int_0^\infty ||e^{-A\tau}||_2 d\tau = \int_0^\infty e^{\alpha\tau} d\tau = -\frac{1}{\alpha} < \infty.$$

In the case $n > 1$, we can split the integral as follows:

$$\int_0^\infty ||e^{-A\tau}||_2 d\tau = \int_0^1 ||e^{-A\tau} d||_2 \tau + \int_1^\infty ||e^{-A\tau}||_2 d\tau.$$

Note that for $\tau \geq 1$ and $n \geq 1$,

$$M_s(\tau) = \sum_{k=0}^{n-1} \frac{||N\tau||_2^k}{k!} = 1 + \sum_{k=1}^{n-1} \frac{||N||_2^k}{k!}\tau^k \geq 1 + \sum_{k=1}^{n-1} \frac{||N||_2^k}{k!}.$$

Let us denote

$$\beta = 1 + \sum_{k=1}^{n-1} \frac{||N||_2^k}{k!},$$

then

$$M_s(\tau) \geq \beta,\ M_s(\tau) \geq 1,\ \beta \geq 1.$$

It is easy to see that for $\alpha < 0$,

$$e^{\alpha\tau M_s(\tau)} \leq e^{\alpha\tau\beta},$$

and

$$\int_1^\infty ||e^{-A\tau} d||_2 \tau \leq \int_1^\infty e^{\alpha\tau M_s(\tau)} d\tau \leq \int_1^\infty e^{\alpha\tau\beta} d\tau = -\frac{e^{\alpha\beta}}{\alpha\beta} < \infty.$$

This completes the proof.

If our system has not all but some unstable eigenvalues, this system has a subsystem with the bounded controllable region in some subspace of R^n (obtained for example via the Schur decomposition), and we cannot stabilize the system in the whole state-space.

2.2 Controllable region analysis: known approaches

The controllable region of a linear system defined in (2.1) with only amplitude control constraints has been studied by Formalsky (Formalsky, 1968), Goman et al. (Goman et al., 1996; Goman and Demenkov, 2004*b*), Hu and Lin (Hu and Lin, 2001*b*) (in the latter work the controllable region is called the *asymptotically null controllable region*). Several geometrical properties of the controllable region have been revealed in these works and some methods for explicit characterization of the controllable region have been proposed.

Computation of the controllable region C can be performed by reconstruction of its boundary ∂C formed by an invariant manifold of system trajectories under the bang-bang control (Goman et al., 1996; Hu and Lin, 2001*b*). It has been shown that trajectories on ∂C satisfy Pontryagin's minimum principle (Pontryagin, Boltyanskii, Gamkrelidze and Mishchenko, 1962) and can contain unstable equilibrium points and closed orbits (Goman et al., 1996; Hu and Lin, 2001*b*).

The boundaries of stability and controllable regions for a two-dimensional system with only anti-stable eigenvalues and scalar limited control input have been analyzed in (Goman et al., 1996) considering the bang-bang control. The geometric properties of the boundary trajectories have been investigated using bifurcation analysis methods. Later similar results have been independently obtained in (Hu and Lin, 2001*b*) with the rigorous proof of the boundary trajectories properties.

Every continuous linear system can be approximated with an arbitrary precision by a discrete-time one. For the linear discrete-time system it is then possible to approximate its controllable region with an arbitrary precision by the set of linear inequalities using numeric techniques proposed in (Gutman and Cwikel, 1987; Keerthi and Gilbert, 1987; Lasserre, 1993; Mayne and Schroeder, 1997). The methods of approximation are mainly based on the Fourier-Motzkin elimination or on the convex hull computing techniques. Since we use the discretization of the system in our own algorithm, we briefly consider these *polyhedral* methods below.

2.2.1 Polyhedral methods of controllable region computation

We will focus our attention on the anti-stable subsystem (i.e. having only anti-stable open-loop eigenvalues) of our linear unstable system. We suppose that system has no neutral subspace.

For simplicity of notations, we can write this subsystem in the same form:

$$\dot{x}(t) = Ax(t) + Bu(t), \tag{2.3}$$

where $x \in R^n$ and $u \in R^m$.

Let the control $u \in U$ be constrained as

$$|u^{(i)}| \leq u^{(i)}_{max}. \tag{2.4}$$

As we know from the previous section, the controllable region C in this case is convex and bounded set. The idea is to approximate C by linear inequality system, because any bounded and convex set can be approximated by linear inequalities with arbitrary precision.

We restrict our attention to the set of all piecewise constant control functions of the form:

$$u^{(i)}(t) = u_k^{(i)},\ t \in [k\Delta T, (k+1)\Delta T], \tag{2.5}$$

where k is integer value, started from 0. Here and below we will denote as uk and xk the values of control and state vector at the sample time $t = k\Delta T$. It is clear that if $|u_k^{(i)}| \leq u^{(i)}_{max}$ for every k, then constraints (2.4) hold for all the time t.

One can form an augmented system on the sampling time interval:

$$\dot{\psi}(t) = M\psi(t), M = \begin{bmatrix} A & B \\ 0 & 0 \end{bmatrix}, \psi = \begin{bmatrix} x \\ u \end{bmatrix},$$

with initial condition vector of $\psi_k = [x_k\,;\, u_k]$. Then it is easy to compute the matrix exponential $\Phi = e^{M\Delta T}$ such that $\psi_k+1 = \Phi\psi_k$. This matrix Φ has the following structure:

$$\Phi = \begin{bmatrix} F & G \\ 0 & 1 \end{bmatrix}.$$

The submatrices F and G of matrix Φ, which correspond to the state vector x_k and to the control input u_k, form the state-space representation of the discrete-time system, which is derived from the continuous-time one:

$$x_{k+1} = Fx_k + Gu_k \tag{2.6}$$

with the constraint

$$|u_k| \leq u_{max}. \tag{2.7}$$

It is important to note that the origin of system (2.6) corresponds to the equilibrium point of system (2.3) with $x(t) = 0$ and $u(t) = 0$. As ΔT approaches zero, the behaviours of two systems converge. So, we focus our attention on system (2.6), trying to approximate the controllable region of system (2.3) by the controllable region of (2.6).

2.2.2 Construction of null-controllable sets

Definition 2 *A k-step null-controllable set C(k) with respect to the system (2.6) is the set of all initial states, from which it is possible to reach the origin by applying any k-length control sequence constrained by (2.7).*

Note that an *isochrone* for a continuous-time system is defined as the surface of a null-controllable set for the discrete-time system. The surface of a k-step null-controllable set corresponds to the isochrone for a continuous time of $k\Delta T$.

Definition 3 *A one-step controllable set to a region with respect to the system (2.6) is the set of all initial states, from which it is possible to reach the region in one step by applying any control constrained by (2.7).*

The focus of this section is the algorithm for constructing the null-controllable set via a one-step controllable set to a region, a method first introduced in (Keerthi and Gilbert, 1987).

Let us consider a polyhedral region C_0 in the state-space, defined by the set of linear inequalities of the form:

$$C_0 = \{x \in R^n \,|\, a_i x \leq c_i,\ i = \overline{1, N}\}. \tag{2.8}$$

with the given row vector a_i and scalars c_i.

Given a set of the form (2.8), the one-step controllable set to C_0 is the projection of a set C^* onto a subspace, which is orthogonal to the control variable, where

$$C^* = \{[x; u] \in R^{(n+m)} : u \in U,\ Fx + Gu \in C_0\},$$

and this C^* is given by a linear inequality set of the form

$$a_i Fx + a_i Gu \leq c_i,\ i = \overline{1, N};$$

$$-u_{max} \leq u \leq u_{max}.$$

The projection C_1 of C^* is in the same form as (2.8) and it can be computed via the Fourier-Motzkin elimination method, i.e. by eliminating from C^* the control variable. Then, the set C_1 defines the polyhedron in the state-space, containing all of the points from which it is possible to drive the system in one step into C_0.

The initial set has the form of *any* linear inequality set, containing the origin only. Then, after applying the elimination method, we have a 1-step null-controllable set. But, the one-step controllable set to a 1-step null-controllable set is exactly the 2-step null-controllable set. Proceeding in the same way, we can construct a sequence of nested polyhedrons.

Let us denote as $L(\cdot)$ the procedure of a one-step controllable set construction. Then any k-step null-controllable set is defined as

$$C(k) = L(C(k-1)).$$

It is known that in unstable subspace the controllable region is convex and bounded. Because of this it is possible to stop this process after convergence of i-step null-controllable sets to the boundary of the controllable region (see Fig. 2.1).

Now we briefly discuss the elimination method, proposed in (Keerthi and Gilbert, 1987) for controllable regions computation.

2.2.3 Fourier-Motzkin method

The Fourier-Motzkin elimination method (FME) can be used to eliminate variables in a linear inequality system, in a step by step manner, by constructing a series of inequalities (see (Dantzig, 1966)). This method may be regarded as an extension of the Gaussian elimination method for a system of linear equations. In (Dantzig, 1966) the FME is used to discuss the linear programming (LP) problems, and the LP example is investigated. There are many applications of the FME (for examples, see (Chandru, 1993; Duffin, 1974; Kohler, 1967)).

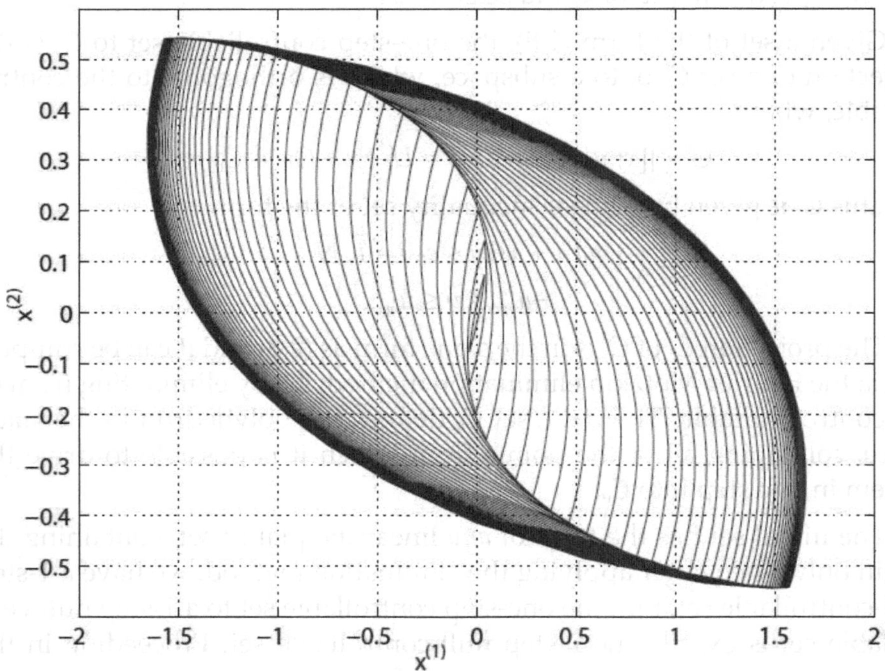

Figure 2.1: Convergence of null-controllable sets

A brief method description is as follows.

Suppose that we have a system of linear inequalities of the form:

$$a_i x + b_i u \le c_i,\ i = \overline{1, N}, \qquad (2.9)$$

where a_i is row vector, x denotes column vector of variables and u denotes scalar variable, which we would like to eliminate from the system. Let us denote as I_+ the set of all i indices corresponding to $b_i > 0$, and in the same way I_- denotes the similar set for $b_i < 0$. Zero coefficient indexes are collected in the set I_0.

Let us divide these inequalities into three groups defined by I_+,I_- and I_0 sets. Consider the groups corresponding to I_+ and I_- in slightly modified form:

$$-\frac{a_i}{b_i}x + \frac{c_i}{b_i} \le u, i \in I_-; \quad u \le -\frac{a_j}{b_j}x + \frac{c_j}{b_j}, j \in I_+$$

For eliminating the variable u let us sequentially replace u in each inequality from I_- by right side of all inequalities from I_+. Then the projection of the polyhedron onto subspace of x defined by (2.9) is given by

$$\left(\frac{a_j}{b_j} - \frac{a_i}{b_i}\right) x \le \left(\frac{c_j}{b_j} - \frac{c_i}{b_i}\right), j \in I_+, i \in I_-;$$
$$a_l x \le c_l, l \in I_0.$$

This method may be very time consuming and memory crucial due to producing a growing number of hyperplanes. However, most of them can be excluded from the description by using the linear programming. Suppose that we have linear inequality system

$$a_i x \le c_i,\ i = \overline{1, N} \qquad (2.9)$$

and we have to check the j-th inequality for redundancy. Consider the following linear programming task:

$$a_j \to max,$$
$$a_i x \le c_i,\ i = \overline{1, N}, i \ne j.$$

Then, compare the solution of this problem with c_j. The solution greater than c_j indicates non-redundant inequality.

2.2.4 Formalsky's method

An optimization-based method for explicit description of the controllable region boundary has been first proposed by A.M. Formalsky in (Formalsky, 1968), and then applied to the investigation of linear unstable systems in his book (Formalsky, 1974). To the author's knowledge, it was the first book in the world that systematically addresses problems associated with limited controllable and stability regions. Recently, the method has been rediscovered in (Hu, Lin and Qiu, 2002; Hu and Lin, 2001*b*) for the case of continuous systems. In (Hu, Miller and Qiu, 2002) a counterpart for discrete-time systems has been outlined.

Let us consider the anti-stable subsystem under amplitude control constraints. The main idea of the method is based on the maximization of a scalar linear function $f(z) = d^T z$ ($d \in R^n$, $d \neq 0$) over all points z from the controllable region. The maximization process is performed along the specified direction d, so that the final solution coincides with the point z_d on the boundary of the controllable region. Since the controllable region for anti-stable system with only amplitude constraints is strictly convex and overall bounded, this solution always exists and it is unique. The vector d defines supporting hyperplane at this boundary point zd. Also we suppose for simplicity that $u^{(i)}_{max} = -u^{(i)}_{min}$.

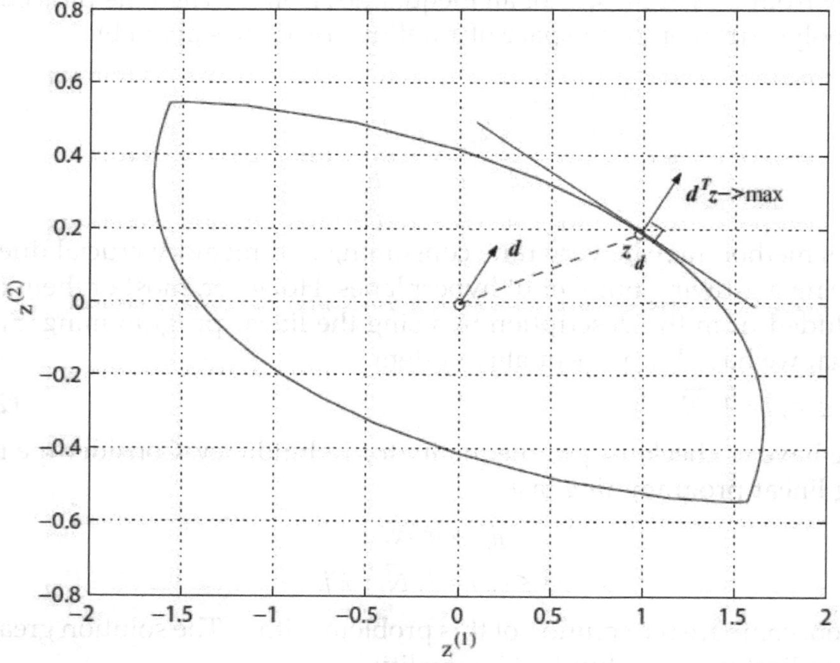

Figure 2.2: Formalsky's method

To compute the controllable region boundary, let us consider a *null-controllable* set C(*T*) of all points in the state-space, from which the system can be moved to the origin at the presence of control constraints in a time less than or equal to T. Note that the controllability region boundary corresponds to the boundary of $C(\infty)$.

The points in a *null-controllable* set $C(T)$ can be expressed explicitly as initial points $z(0)$ for the Cauchy problem through the applied control function $u(t)$ on the time interval $[0, T]$. The general solution of system (3.1):

$$z(T) = e^{A_z T} z(0) + \int_0^T e^{A_z (T-t)} B_z u(t)dt, z(T) = 0$$

transporting the system to the origin can be transformed as:

$$C(T) = \{z | z = - \int_0^T e^{-A_z t} B_z u(t)dt, u(t) \in U\}.$$

The optimization task for maximizing a linear function $d^T z$ on $C(T)$ has only one solution z_d:

$$z_d = \arg \max_{z \in C(T)} d^T z = - \sum_{i=1}^{m} \int_0^T e^{-A_z t} b_{zi} u_{max}^{(i)} \text{sign}(-d^T e^{-A_z t} b_{zi})dt,$$

where b_{zi} is a column of matrix B_z.

For two-dimensional systems, computing boundary points zd_l of a *null-controllable* set $C(T)$ for a number of different directions d_l

$$d_l =| [\cos \varphi_l, \sin \varphi_l]^T; \ \varphi_l = \frac{2\pi k}{N}, \ l = \overline{1, N}$$

we can approximate $C(T)$ rather accurately. For systems of higher dimension, the proposed method requires generation of too many direction vectors, but it is still useful as an idea to discover properties of controllable region boundary.

Considering a sequence of $T_i = T_{i-1} + \Delta T$ approaching infinity $T_i \to \infty$ we will have $C(T_i) \to C$. This convergence process can be stopped if

$$\max_l ||z_{d_l}(T_i) - z_{d_l}(T_{i-1})||_2 \leq \epsilon,$$

where ΔT is a small time increment and ∈ is required accuracy.

2.3 Computation of controllable region slices

In the sequel, we will slightly modify the definition of controllable region so that we can use rate constraints as well in our derivation of the computational algorithm. Basically, it holds the same properties as the region for the case of only amplitude constraints. Convexity can be demonstrated in the same way as we have done it in Theorem 1.

We will study the effect on system dynamics of the following constraints:

$$u_{min} \le u \le u_{max}, \tag{2.11a}$$

$$\dot{u}_{min} \le \dot{u} \le \dot{u}_{max}. \tag{2.11b}$$

Here the inequalities are treated componentwise.

We say that an extended state $[x_0; u_0]$ is asymptotically null controllable if there exists a control function $u(t)$ that satisfies constraints in (2.11) and generates the state trajectory with initial conditions $x(0) = x_0$ and $u(0) = u_0$, so that the state and control asymptotically approach the origin as $t \to \infty$:

$$\lim_{t\to\infty} x(t) = 0, \ \lim_{t\to\infty} u(t) = 0. \tag{2.12}$$

We will call the set of all extended states $[x_0; u_0] \in R^{n+m}$ that are asymptotically null controllable again the *controllable region* for the system and denote it by $C \in R^{n+m}$.

2.3.1 Key idea

Two unit vectors e_i and e_j directed along the i-th and j-th axes of coordinate system in R^{n+m} space form a basis in the slice plane $SL(i, j)$. Any point in this plane can be expressed as a linear combination of e_i and e_j:

$$SL(i, j) = \{[x_0; u_0] \in R^{n+m} \text{ so that } [x_0; u_0] = \xi_1 e_i + \xi_2 e_j\}, \tag{2.13}$$

where ξ_1, ξ_2 are scalar variables.

Then the cross-section $\Xi(i, j)$ of the controllable region C by plane $SL(i, j)$ in coordinates ξ_1 and ξ_2 is defined as:

$$\Xi(i, j) = \{\xi \in R^2 \text{ so that } [x_0; u_0] \in SL(i, j) \cap C\}, \tag{2.14}$$

where $\xi = [\xi_1, \xi_2]^T$.

From the convexity of C it follows that $\Xi(i, j)$ is also a convex set.

The key idea of the algorithm results from the observation that each point on the boundary of the controllable region cross-section is a solution of the optimization task, in which a linear function is maximized over the set of points belonging both to the controllable region and the slice plane. This idea is clearly a modification of the explicit method described above, but instead of the explicit formula the solution is based on a method of numerical optimization.

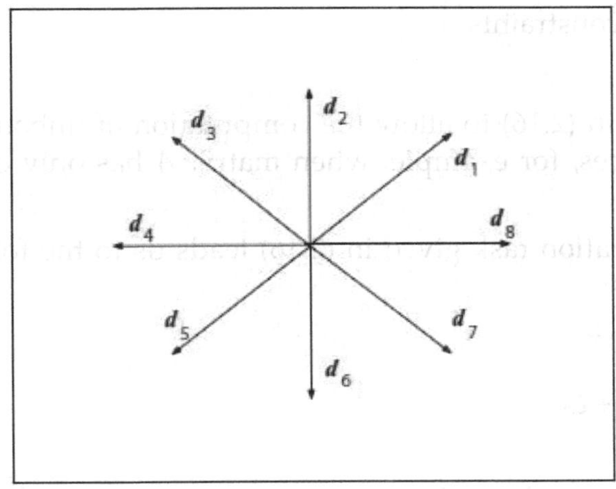

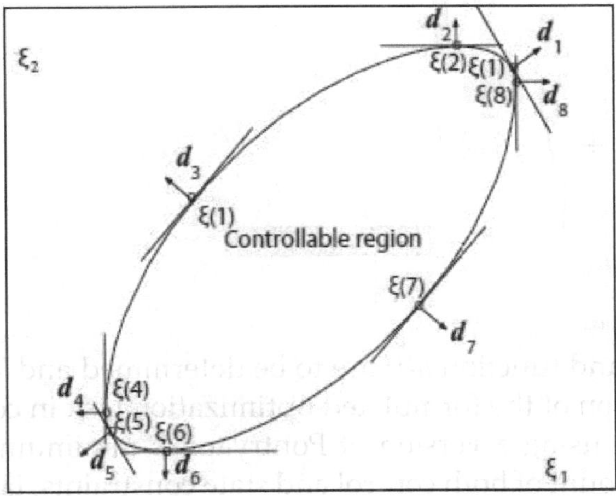

Figure 2.3: The key idea of the algorithm : maximization of the linear function over the controllable region.

To approximate the boundary of the controllable region let us consider a set of vectors d_l in the plane $SL(i, j)$ uniformly distributed from the centre in different directions (see Fig. 2.3, top plot):

$$d_l = [\cos \varphi_l, \sin \varphi_l]^T, \varphi_l = 2\pi l/M, l = 1, ..., M. \tag{2.15}$$

Then the points $\xi(l)$ belonging to the boundary of the controllable region in the slice $SL(i, j)$ will be defined as the solutions of the following optimization task (see Fig. 2.3, bottom plot):

$$\xi(l) = \arg \max_{\substack{\xi \in \Xi(i,j) \\ \xi \geq \xi_{min} \\ \xi \leq \xi_{max}}} (d_l^T \xi). \tag{2.16}$$

The additional constraints

$$\xi_{min} \leq \xi \leq \xi_{max} \tag{2.17}$$

are introduced in (2.16) to allow the computation of unbounded controllable region slices, for example, when matrix A has only one anti-stable eigenvalue.

The optimization task given in (2.16) leads us to the following variational equations:

$$d_l^T \xi \rightarrow \max \tag{2.18a}$$

$$[x_0; u_0] = \xi_1 e_i + \xi_2 e_j \tag{2.18b}$$

$$x_0 = -\int_0^T e^{-A\tau} Bu(\tau)d\tau \tag{2.18c}$$

$$u(\tau) = u_0 + \int_0^\tau \dot{u}(t)dt \tag{2.18d}$$

$$u_{min} \leq u(\tau) \leq u_{max} \tag{2.18e}$$

$$\dot{u}_{min} \leq \dot{u}(t) \leq \dot{u}_{max} \tag{2.18f}$$

where vector ξ and function $\dot{u}(t)$ are to be determined and T is sufficiently large. The solution of the formulated optimization task in continuous time can be obtained using a version of Pontryagin's minimum principle that takes proper account of both control and state constraints. However, due to computational difficulties in the application of the minimum principle, in this chapter we use a different method that is based on a discrete approximation of the formulated problem.

2.3.2 Discretization

To solve numerically the optimization task defined by (2.16), the control function $u(t)$ is parameterized with sampling time ΔT and the system defined in (2.1) is treated as a discrete one. In this case the powerful linear programming methods can be applied to solve the optimization problem.

Let continuous piecewise-linear control function be in the following form:

$$u(t) = uk + \dot{u}_k(t - k\Delta T) \text{ for } t \in [k\Delta T, (k+1)\Delta T]. \quad (2.19)$$

Here $k \geq 0$ is an integer value, $u_k \in R^m$ denotes the control vector and $\dot{u}_k \in R^m$ denotes the vector of control inputs rates at time instant $t = k\Delta T$.

It is clear that if

$$u_{min} \leq u_k \leq u_{max}, \quad (2.20a)$$

$$\dot{u}_{min} \leq \dot{u}_k \leq \dot{u}_{max}, \quad (2.20b)$$

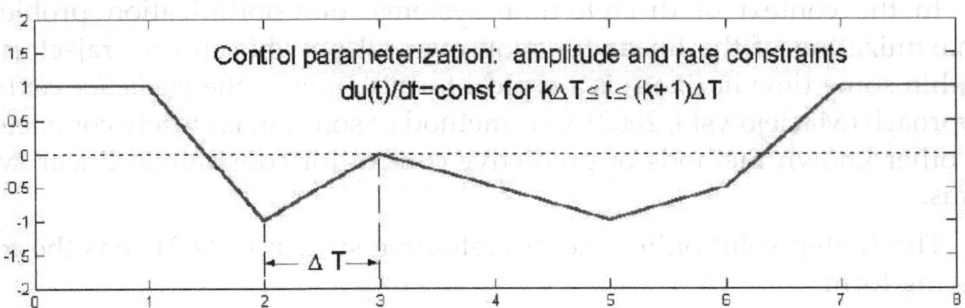

Figure 2.4: Parameterization of the control function

for all k, then both amplitude and rate control constraints in (2.11) hold for all t (see Fig. 2.4).

It is possible to express the state and control vectors at time instant $t = (k+1)\Delta T$ as functions of x_k, u_k and $\dot{u}_k$ using the matrix exponential. As a result, the following discrete system is constructed:

$$x_{k+1} = Fx_k + Gu_k + H\dot{u}_k, \quad (2.21a)$$

$$u_{k+1} = u_k + \dot{u}_k \Delta T. \quad (2.21b)$$

where $F = e^{A\Delta T} \in R^{n\times n}$, $G = \int_0^{\Delta T} e^{A(\Delta T-\tau)} Bd\tau \in R^{n\times m}$, $H = \int_0^{\Delta T} e^{A(\Delta T-\tau)} B\tau d\tau \in R^{n\times m}$ and x_k is the system state at the time instant $t = k\Delta T$.

2.3.3 Predictive equations for discrete-time system

The controllable or null controllable region for the discrete system in (2.21) can be defined similarly to the continuous-time system case. Namely, C is the set of all extended states $[x_0; u_0]$ that can be driven to the origin by the control sequence constrained by (2.20).

The null-controllable set at step N, denoted as $C(N)$, is the set of extended states $[x_0; u_0]$ that can be steered to the origin with admissible control in N steps. It is clear by definition that the region $C(N)$ is a subset of the null-controllable set at time $N\Delta T$ for the continuous-time system.

As for the continuous system, all eigenvalues λ_i, $i = 1, ..., n$ of matrix F in (2.21) can be divided into stable ($|\lambda_i| < 1$), neutral ($|\lambda_i| = 1$) and anti-stable ($|\lambda_i| > 1$) groups. Here $|\lambda_i|$ is the complex modulus of λ_i.

The controllable region for the continuous-time system in (2.1) can be approximated by the null-controllable set at step N for its discrete-time counterpart in (2.21) with sufficiently small sampling time ΔT and large N. The number of steps N specifies the number of unknown variables in an optimization procedure. For better approximation it is necessary to take N as large as possible.

In the context of discrete-time systems, our optimization problem (maximization of the linear function over all possible future trajectories within some time horizon) is a typical formulation of the *predictive control* approach (Maciejowski, 2002). Our method of solution is closely connected to other known methods of predictive control for constrained linear systems.

The N-step solution for the discrete-time system in (2.21) has the following form:

$$x_N = F^N x_0 + \sum_{k=0}^{N-1} F^{N-k-1}(Gu_k + H\dot{u}_k), \tag{2.22a}$$

$$u_N = u_0 + \Delta T \sum_{k=0}^{N-1} \dot{u}_k, \tag{2.22b}$$

where x_0 is the initial state vector and u_0 is the initial control vector for the discrete system.

The following combination of predictive equations (2.22) with control constraints (2.20) and terminal conditions ($x_N = 0$, $u_N = 0$) describes all the initial states $[x_0; u_0] \in C(N)$ for which there exists an admissible sequence of control input rates $\dot{u}_0, ..., \dot{u}_{N-1}$:

$$F^N x_0 + \sum_{k=0}^{N-1} F^{N-k-1}(Gu_k + H\dot{u}_k) = 0, \tag{2.23a}$$

$$u_k = u_0 + \Delta T \sum_{r=0}^{k-1} \dot{u}_r, \; k = \overline{1, N}, \tag{2.23b}$$

$$u_{min} \le u_k \le u_{max}, \; \dot{u}_{min} \le \dot{u}_k \le \dot{u}_{max}, \; k = \overline{0, N-1} \tag{2.23c}$$

$$u_N = 0. \tag{2.23d}$$

Unfortunately, (2.23a) is ill-conditioned if matrix F has anti-stable eigenvalues (Rossiter, Kouvaritakis and Rice, 1998). The computational difficulties in this case follow from the computation of matrix F^k leading to very large errors as k increases.

When matrix F has no stable or neutral eigenvalues (2.23a) can be multiplied by F^{-N} and made well-conditioned:

$$x_0 = -\sum_{k=0}^{N-1} F^{-k-1}(Gu_k + H\dot{u}_k), \tag{2.24}$$

because matrix F^{-k} in this case has no anti-stable eigenvalues. However when matrix F has both stable and anti-stable eigenvalues matrix F^{-k} also has both types of eigenvalues and to improve numerical conditioning via matrix inversion is not further possible.

In (Rossiter et al., 1998) a prestabilization procedure has been proposed to avoid the onset of very large errors in matrices of the form F^k. In this chapter a method based on system decomposition is implemented to avoid the numerical ill-conditioning problem.

2.3.4 Decomposition of discrete-time system

We will use again the Schur decomposition for matrix F. Consider the following transformation of the state-space basis in (2.21):

$$X = [Q_\zeta \mid Q_z]\begin{bmatrix} \zeta \\ z \end{bmatrix} \tag{2.25}$$

so that $[Q_\zeta \mid Q_z]^T [Q_\zeta \mid Q_z] = I$. The columns of $Q_\zeta \in R^{n\times(n-q)}$ span the subspace V_ζ associated with $(n-q)$ stable and neutral eigenvalues, while the columns of $Q_z \in R^{n\times q}$ span the subspace V_z, which is a complementary subspace of V_ζ. Note that $V_z \cup V_\zeta = R^n$ and V_ζ is an F-invariant subspace, i.e. from $x \in V_\zeta$ it follows that $F_x \in V_\zeta$.

In the new basis the open-loop system in (2.21) is represented as

$$\begin{bmatrix} \zeta_{k+1} \\ z_{k+1} \end{bmatrix} = Q^T F Q \begin{bmatrix} \zeta_k \\ z_k \end{bmatrix} + Q^T G u_k + Q^T H \dot{u}_k =$$

$$\begin{bmatrix} Q_\zeta^T F Q_\zeta & Q_\zeta^T F Q_z \\ 0_{q\times(n-q)} & Q_z^T F Q_z \end{bmatrix}\begin{bmatrix} \zeta_k \\ z_k \end{bmatrix} + \begin{bmatrix} Q_\zeta^T G \\ Q_z^T G \end{bmatrix} u_k + \begin{bmatrix} Q_\zeta^T H \\ Q_z^T H \end{bmatrix} \dot{u}_k, \tag{2.26}$$

where matrix $Q^T{}_\zeta F Q_\zeta$ has only stable and neutral eigenvalues, matrix $Q^T{}_z F Q_z$ has only anti-stable eigenvalues and together these eigenvalues form the whole spectrum of eigenvalues for matrix F.

Note that z_k dynamics associated with q anti-stable eigenvalues is decoupled from ζ_k and described by the following open-loop subsystem:

$$z_{k+1} = F_z z_k + G_z u_k + H_z \dot{u}_k, \tag{2.27}$$

where $F_z = Q^T_z F Q_z \in R^{q\times q}$, $G_z = Q^T_z G \in R^{q\times m}$, $H_z = Q^T_z H \in R^{q\times m}$ and $z_k = Q^T_z x_k$.

In a similar way the transformation of the state-space basis can decouple the dynamics associated with stable and neutral eigenvalues. Consider the following transformation of the basis in (2.21):

$$x = [Q_w \mid Q_s]\begin{bmatrix} w \\ s \end{bmatrix} \tag{2.28}$$

so that $[Q_w \mid Q_s]^T [Q_w \mid Q_s] = I$. The columns of $Q_w \in R^{n\times q}$ span the subspace V_w associated with q anti-stable eigenvalues and the columns of $Q_s \in R^{n\times(n-q)}$ span the complementary subspace V_s of V_w. Obviously, $V_w \cup V_s = R_n$ and V_w is an F -invariant subspace.

Dynamics associated with the stable and neutral eigenvalues s_k can be isolated similar to anti-stable eigenvalues case (see (2.27)):

$$s_{k+1} = F_s s_k + G_s u_k + H_s \dot{u}_k, \tag{2.29}$$

where $F_s = Q^T_s F Q_s \in R^{(n-q)\times(n-q)}$, $G_s = Q^T_s G \in R^{(n-q)\times m}$, $H_s = Q^T_s H \in R^{(n-q)\times m}$ and $s_k = Q^T_s x_k$.

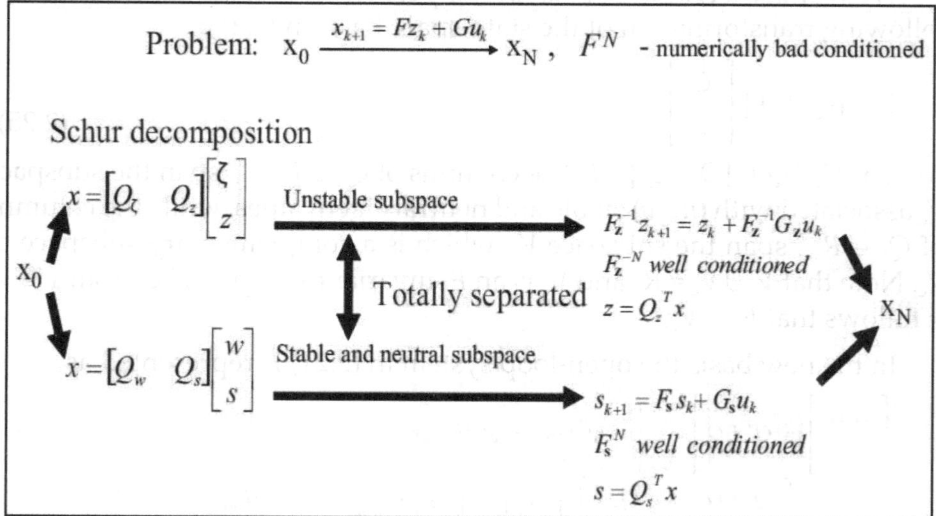

Figure 2.5: The idea of numerically robust prediction

2.3.5 Numerically robust solution via linear programming

The decomposed subsystems for anti-stable and stable/neutral subspaces (see (2.27) and (2.29)) allow the construction of well conditioned predictive equations for z and s, respectively:

$$F_z^{-N} z_N = z_0 + \sum_{k=0}^{N-1} F_z^{-k-1}(G_z u_k + H_z \dot{u}_k), \tag{2.30a}$$

$$s_N = F_s^N s_0 + \sum_{k=0}^{N-1} F_s^{N-k-1}(G_s u_k + H_s \dot{u}_k). \tag{2.30b}$$

The underlying idea here (illustrated in Fig. 2.5) is that matrices F_z^{-k} and F_s^k are well-conditioned, because both F_z^{-1} and Fs do not contain anti-stable eigenvalues and large errors in F_z^{-k} and F_s^k do not appear.

Note that the evolution of the full state vector x_k is completely defined by the evolution of the subsystems states s_k and z_k.

The ultimate goal of the computational algorithm is to maximize the following scalar function for every given vector $d_l \in R^2$ in the slice plane $SL(i, j)$:

$$d_l^T \xi \to \max, \tag{2.31}$$

so that points $[x_0; u_0] = \xi_1 e_i + \xi_2 e_j$ belong to the controllable region $C(N)$. The resulting vector $\xi(l)$ will define a point on the boundary of the controllable region (see Fig. 2.3).

To specify this optimization problem we need to combine the well-conditioned predictive equations (2.30) with terminal conditions $s_N = 0$, $z_N = 0$, add initial conditions $s_0 = Q_s^T x_0$, $z_0 = Q_z^T x_0$, control constraints (2.20) and confine the allowable area in the plane $SL(i, j)$ to consider unbounded controllable regions. All these form the following set of linear constraints:

$$Q_z^T(\xi_1 e_{xi} + \xi_2 e_{xj}) = -\sum_{k=0}^{N-1} F_z^{-k-1}(G_z u_k + H_z \dot{u}_k), \tag{2.32a}$$

$$F_s^N Q_s^T(\xi_1 e_{xi} + \xi_2 e_{xj}) = -\sum_{k=0}^{N-1} F_s^{N-k-1}(G_s u_k + H_s \dot{u}_k), \tag{2.32b}$$

$$u_k = u_0 + \Delta T \sum_{r=0}^{k-1} \dot{u}_r, \; k = \overline{1, N}, \tag{2.32c}$$

$$u_0 = \xi_1 e_{ui} + \xi_2 e_{uj}, \; u_N = 0, \tag{2.32d}$$

$$u_{min} \le u_k \le u_{max}, \; \dot{u}_{min} \le \dot{u}_k \le \dot{u}_{max}, \; k = \overline{0, N-1} \tag{2.32e}$$

$$\xi_{min} \leq \xi \leq \xi_{max}. \tag{2.32f}$$

where unit vector $e_i \in R^{n+m}$ is resolved on the state ($e_{xi} \in R^n$) and the control ($e_{ui} \in R_m$) vector components: $e_i = [e_{xi}; e_{ui}]$.

The unknown variables in the set of linear constraints in (2.32) are the coordinate vector in the slice plane $\xi = [\xi 1, \xi 2]^T$ and the control rate vectors $\dot{u}_k$, $k = \overline{0, N-1}$.

The optimization problem formulated above can be effectively solved by a linear programming method.

2.3.6 Computational issues

All computational results presented in this chapter have been obtained using MATLAB 6.5 on a personal computer Pentium IV 1.6GHz. For example, the computation of the boundary of the controllable region for an eight-dimensional dynamical system considered as an example in the next section takes 20 seconds when $N = 100$ (only amplitude constraints have been imposed). For the Schur decomposition of the discrete systems the function *blkrsch* from the Robust Control Toolbox (MathWorks, 2001*b*) has been used. The linear programming has been performed by the function *linprog* (large-scale algorithm) from the Optimization Toolbox (MathWorks, 2001*a*).

2.4 Numerical examples

Example 1: controllable regions beyond the flutter boundary

The active flutter suppression problem has been intensively investigated with implementation of different control design techniques (Friedmann, 1999; Waszak, 1998; Waszak, 2001; Mukhopadhyay, 2000; Frampton and Clark, 2000; Scott and Pado, 2000; Ko, Strganac and Kurdila, 1998; Block and Strganac, 1998; Mukhopadhyay, 2003). Different linear and non-linear controllers applied for flutter suppression improve system's dynamic responses and extend flutter boundary. However, these approaches have difficulty when realistic constraints are imposed on the maximum rate and deflection of the control surfaces used for flutter control. It is indicated (Friedmann, 1999) that there exists some limit in terms of dynamic pressure or flow speed for possible delay of the flutter onset in the closed-loop system.

This fact can be related to the size of the controllable region for the open-loop system beyond the flutter boundary. Due to limited authority of control effectors the size of the controllable region decreases with increase of system instability and can become critical against the level of external disturbances. This view on the flutter suppression problem was pioneered in (Goman and Demenkov, 2004*a*) and then addressed by (Applebaum and Ben-Asher, 2007).

A more deep insight into the active flutter suppression problem will require a detailed analysis of the controllable regions for the open-loop system and regions of attraction for the closed-loop system. Such analysis will help to improve the control laws design and provide the realistic level of robustness for an active control flutter suppression system.

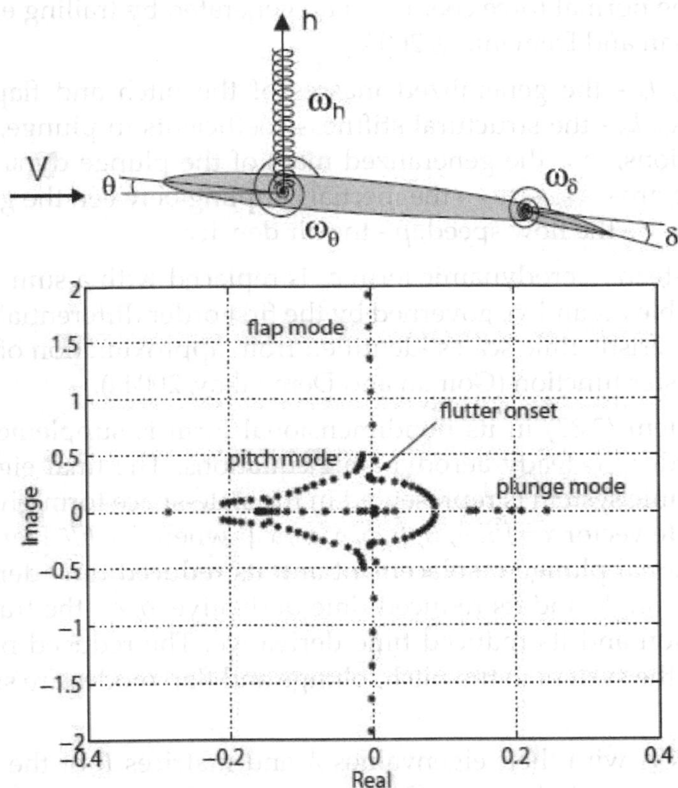

Figure 2.6: Sketch of the aeroservoelastic airfoil system and the root-loci for different reduced frequencies in pitch.

To elucidate the proposed approach we consider hereafter an airfoil with trailing-edge flap, which can be treated as a typical wing section (see Fig.2.6).

The dynamic equations of this aeroservoelastic system can be represented in the follow-ing matrix form(Goman and Demenkov, 2004*a*):

$$\begin{bmatrix} m_a & s_{h\theta} & s_{h\delta} \\ s_{h\delta} & I_\theta & s_{\theta\delta} \\ s_{h\delta} & s_{\theta\delta} & I_\delta \end{bmatrix} \begin{bmatrix} \ddot{h} \\ \ddot{\theta} \\ \ddot{\delta} \end{bmatrix} + \begin{bmatrix} k_h & 0 & 0 \\ 0 & k_\theta & 0 \\ 0 & 0 & k_\delta \end{bmatrix} \begin{bmatrix} h \\ \theta \\ \delta \end{bmatrix} = \begin{bmatrix} 0 \\ 0 \\ k_\delta \end{bmatrix} \delta_c + \begin{bmatrix} c_h(\rho U^2/2)S \\ c_m(\rho U^2/2)S\bar{c} \\ c_\delta(\rho U^2/2)S\bar{c} \end{bmatrix}, \quad (2.33)$$

where the non-dimensional aerodynamic coefficients for the normal force c_h, the pitch moment c_m and the flap hinge moment c_δ are expressed as linear functions of $\ddot{\theta}$, $\dot{\theta}$, θ, $\ddot{h}$, $\dot{\theta}$, h, $\ddot{\delta}$, $\dot{\delta}$, δ and unsteady aerodynamic contribution to the normal force coefficient c_w, generated by trailing edge vortex wake (Goman and Demenkov, 2004*a*).

Here I_θ, I_δ - the generalized masses of the pitch and flap dynamic modes, k_h, k_θ, k_δ - the structural stiffness coefficients in plunge, pitch and flap deflections, m_a - the generalized mass of the plunge dynamic mode, S - the wing area, $s_{h\theta}$, $s_{h\delta}$, $s_{\theta\delta}$ - the inertial coupling between the generalized coordinates, V - the flow speed, ρ - the air density.

The unsteady aerodynamic term c_w is replaced with a sum of two dynamic variables x_7 and x_8, governed by the first order differential equations with characteristic time scales identified from approximation of the Theodorsen transfer function (Goman and Demenkov, 2004*a*).

The system (2.33) in its nondimensional form is supplemented with two first order unsteady aerodynamic equations. The final eight-dimensional dynamic system is represented in the state-space form given in (2.1) with the state vector $x = [\bar{h}, \dot{\bar{h}}, \theta, \dot{\theta}, \delta, \dot{\delta}, x_7, x_8]^T$ where $\bar{h} = h/\bar{c}$ Here $\bar{h}$, $\dot{\bar{h}}$ - the nondimensional plunge displacement and its reduced time derivative, θ, $\dot{\theta}$ - the pitch angle and its reduced time derivative, δ, $\dot{\delta}$ - the trailing-edge flap deflection and its reduced time derivative. The reduced natural frequencies of the system in the pitch, plunge and flap modes are specified in Table 1.

Matrices A with their eigenvalues λ and matrices B of the linearized aeroservoelastic airfoil system (2.1) are presented below for four different operational conditions beyond the flutter boundary $\omega_\theta = \omega_{\theta fl}$.

1) $\omega_\theta = 0.9\omega_{\theta fl}$

$$A = \begin{bmatrix} 0 & 1.0000 & 0 & 0 & 0 & 0 & \cdots \\ -0.0849 & -0.0167 & -0.0105 & 0.0095 & 0.0186 & 0.0009 & \cdots \\ 0 & 0 & 0 & 1.0000 & 0 & 0 & \cdots \\ -0.1416 & -0.0387 & -0.1820 & -0.0147 & 1.8038 & -0.0034 & \cdots \\ 0 & 0 & 0 & 0 & 0 & 1.0000 & \cdots \\ 0.0351 & 0.0706 & 0.7735 & 0.1260 & -17.4331 & 0.0009 & \cdots \\ 0 & -1.1944 & 1.1944 & 0.5375 & 0.6567 & 0.0888 & \cdots \\ 0 & -0.2932 & 0.2932 & 0.1319 & 0.1612 & 0.0218 & \cdots \end{bmatrix}$$

$$\begin{matrix} 0 & 0. \\ 0.0053 & 0.0053 \\ 0 & 0. \\ 0.0123 & 0.0123 \\ 0 & 0. \\ -0.0225 & -0.0225 \\ -0.8598 & 0. \\ 0 & -0.1673 \end{matrix}\Bigg] \quad B = \begin{bmatrix} 0 \\ -0.0146 \\ 0 \\ -1.8250 \\ 0 \\ 17.5566 \\ 0 \\ 0 \end{bmatrix} \quad \lambda = \begin{bmatrix} -0.0057 \pm 4.1852i \\ -0.0351 \pm 0.3166i \\ 0.0128 \pm 0.2722i \\ -0.1563 \\ -0.8453 \end{bmatrix}$$

2) $\omega_\theta = 0.67\omega_{\theta fl}$

$$A = \begin{bmatrix} 0 & 1.0000 & 0 & 0 & 0 & 0 & \dots \\ -0.0457 & -0.0167 & 0.0021 & 0.0095 & 0.0118 & 0.0009 & \dots \\ 0 & 0 & 0 & 1.0000 & 0 & 0 & \dots \\ -0.0762 & -0.0387 & -0.0800 & -0.0147 & 0.9603 & -0.0034 & \dots \\ 0 & 0 & 0 & 0 & 0 & 1.0000 & \dots \\ 0.0189 & 0.0706 & 0.3834 & 0.1260 & -9.3181 & 0.0009 & \dots \\ 0 & -1.1944 & 1.1944 & 0.5375 & 0.6567 & 0.0888 & \dots \\ 0 & -0.2932 & 0.2932 & 0.1319 & 0.1612 & 0.0218 & \dots \end{bmatrix}$$

$$\begin{matrix} 0 & 0. \\ 0.0053 & 0.0053 \\ 0 & 0. \\ 0.0123 & 0.0123 \\ 0 & 0. \\ -0.0225 & -0.0225 \\ -0.8598 & 0. \\ 0 & -0.1673 \end{matrix}\Bigg] \quad B = \begin{bmatrix} 0 \\ -0.0079 \\ 0 \\ -0.9814 \\ 0 \\ 9.4415 \\ 0 \\ 0 \end{bmatrix} \quad \lambda = \begin{bmatrix} -0.0053 \pm 3.0595i \\ 0.0632 \pm 0.1944i \\ -0.0935 \pm 0.2096i \\ -0.1420 \\ -0.8442 \end{bmatrix}$$

3) $\omega_\theta = 0.42\omega_{\theta fl}$

$$
A = \begin{bmatrix}
0 & 1.0000 & 0 & 0 & 0 & 0 & \dots \\
-0.0185 & -0.0167 & 0.0108 & 0.0095 & 0.0071 & 0.0009 & \dots \\
0 & 0 & 0 & 1.0000 & 0 & 0 & \dots \\
-0.0308 & -0.0387 & -0.0094 & -0.0147 & 0.3763 & -0.0034 & \dots \\
0 & 0 & 0 & 0 & 0 & 1.0000 & \dots \\
0.0077 & 0.0706 & 0.1133 & 0.1260 & -3.7000 & 0.0009 & \dots \\
0 & -1.1944 & 1.1944 & 0.5375 & 0.6567 & 0.0888 & \dots \\
0 & -0.2932 & 0.2932 & 0.1319 & 0.1612 & 0.0218 & \dots
\end{bmatrix}
$$

$$
\begin{matrix}
0 & 0. \\
0.0053 & 0.0053 \\
0 & 0. \\
0.0123 & 0.0123 \\
0 & 0. \\
-0.0225 & -0.0225 \\
-0.8598 & 0. \\
0 & -0.1673
\end{bmatrix}
\quad
B = \begin{bmatrix}
0 \\ -0.0032 \\ 0 \\ -0.3974 \\ 0 \\ 3.8234 \\ 0 \\ 0
\end{bmatrix}
\quad
\lambda = \begin{bmatrix}
-0.0043 \pm 1.9276i \\
0.0842 \pm 0.0865i \\
-0.1531 \pm 0.1154i \\
-0.0665 \\
-0.8445
\end{bmatrix}
$$

4) $\omega_\theta = 0.3\omega_{\theta fl}$

$$A = \begin{bmatrix} 0 & 1.0000 & 0 & 0 & 0 & 0 & \cdots \\ -0.0094 & -0.0167 & 0.0137 & 0.0095 & 0.0056 & 0.0009 & \cdots \\ 0 & 0 & 0 & 1.0000 & 0 & 0 & \cdots \\ -0.0157 & -0.0387 & 0.0142 & -0.0147 & 0.1816 & -0.0034 & \cdots \\ 0 & 0 & 0 & 0 & 0 & 1.0000 & \cdots \\ 0.0039 & 0.0706 & 0.0232 & 0.1260 & -1.8273 & 0.0009 & \cdots \\ 0 & -1.1944 & 1.1944 & 0.5375 & 0.6567 & 0.0888 & \cdots \\ 0 & -0.2932 & 0.2932 & 0.1319 & 0.1612 & 0.0218 & \cdots \end{bmatrix}$$

$$\begin{matrix} 0 & 0. \\ 0.0053 & 0.0053 \\ 0 & 0. \\ 0.0123 & 0.0123 \\ 0 & 0. \\ -0.0225 & -0.0225 \\ -0.8598 & 0. \\ 0 & -0.1673 \end{matrix}\Bigg] \quad B = \begin{bmatrix} 0 \\ -0.0016 \\ 0 \\ -0.2028 \\ 0 \\ 1.9507 \\ 0 \\ 0 \end{bmatrix} \quad \lambda = \begin{bmatrix} -0.0029 \pm 1.3548i \\ -0.1844 \pm 0.0952i \\ 0.1443 \\ 0.0302 \\ -0.0110 \\ -0.8463 \end{bmatrix}$$

The natural frequency in pitch ω_θ is inversely proportional to flow speed as shown in Table 1. The flap mode natural frequency ω_δ in the case considered is much higher than the natural frequency ω_θ and the plunge mode natural frequency ω_h is approximately of the same order (see Table 1).

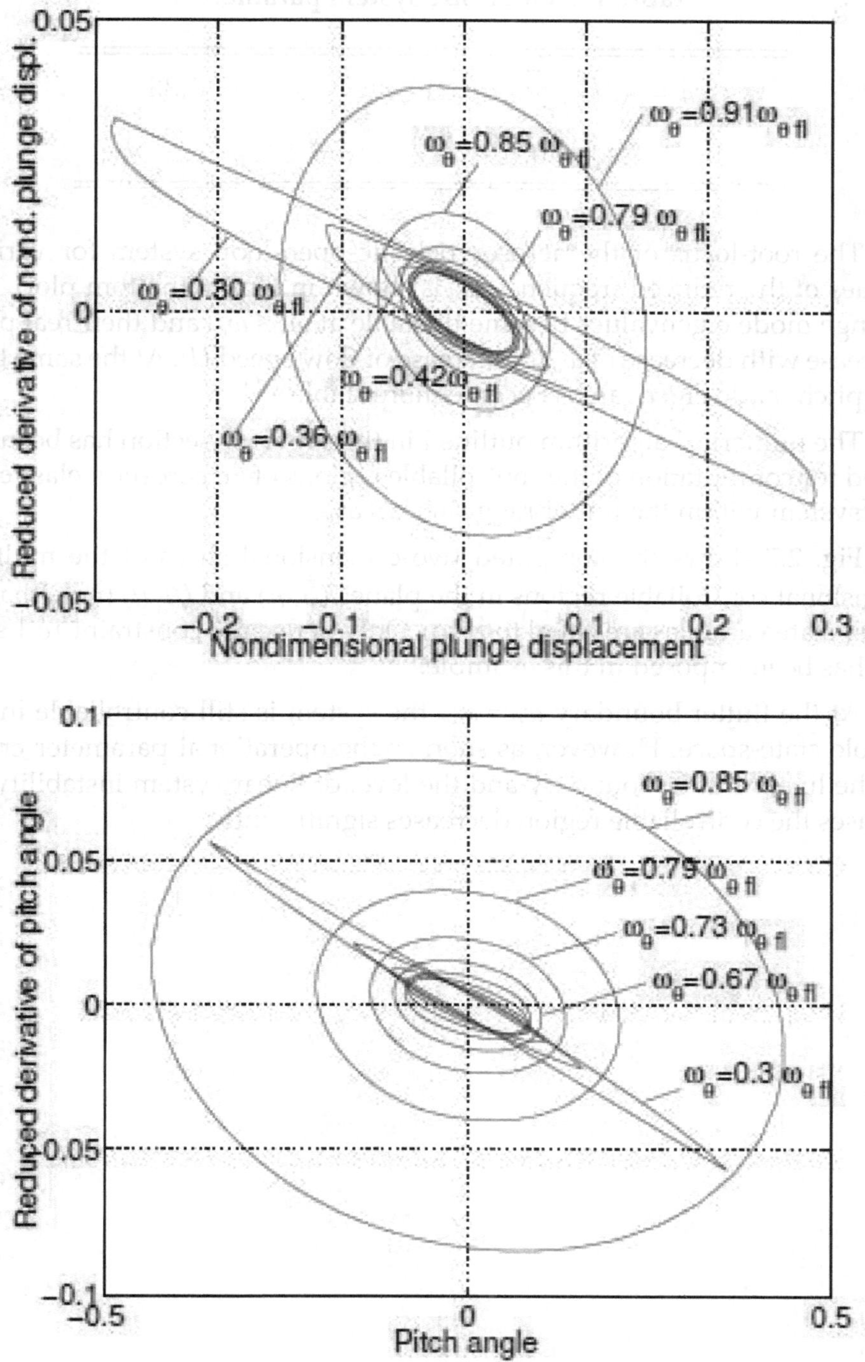

Figure 2.7: Slices of the controllable regions computed for the flutter range of ω_θ under deflection limit $|\delta c| \leq 0.1$ *rad*.

Table 1. Aeroelastic system parameters

$\omega_\theta = \sqrt{k_\theta/m_a}\,\bar{c}/(2V)$,	$\omega_{\theta_{fl}} = 0.33$
$\omega_h = 0.8\omega_\theta$,	$\omega_\delta = 10\omega_\theta$

The root-locus of the aeroservoelastic open-loop system for various values of the reduced frequency ω_θ is shown in Fig.2.6 (bottom plot). The plunge mode eigenvalues become unstable at $\omega_\theta \le \omega_{\theta fl}$ and their real parts increase with decrease of ω_θ (or increase of flow speed U). At the same time the pitch mode eigenvalues become more stable.

The numerical algorithm outlined in the previous section has been applied for computation of the controllable regions of an aeroservoelastic airfoil system within the flutter range at $\omega_\theta \le \omega_{\theta fl}$.

Fig. 2.7 shows the computed two-dimensional slices of the multidimensional controllable regions in the planes $(\dot{\bar{h}}, \bar{h})$ and $(\dot{\theta}, \theta)$ (note that all other state variables are equal to zero). Only deflection constraint $|\delta_c| \le 0.1$ *rad* has been imposed in this example.

At the flutter boundary $\omega_\theta = \omega_{\theta fl}$ the system is still controllable in the whole state-space. However, as soon as the operational parameter crosses the linear flutter boundary and the level of linear system instability increases the controllable region decreases signifi-cantly.

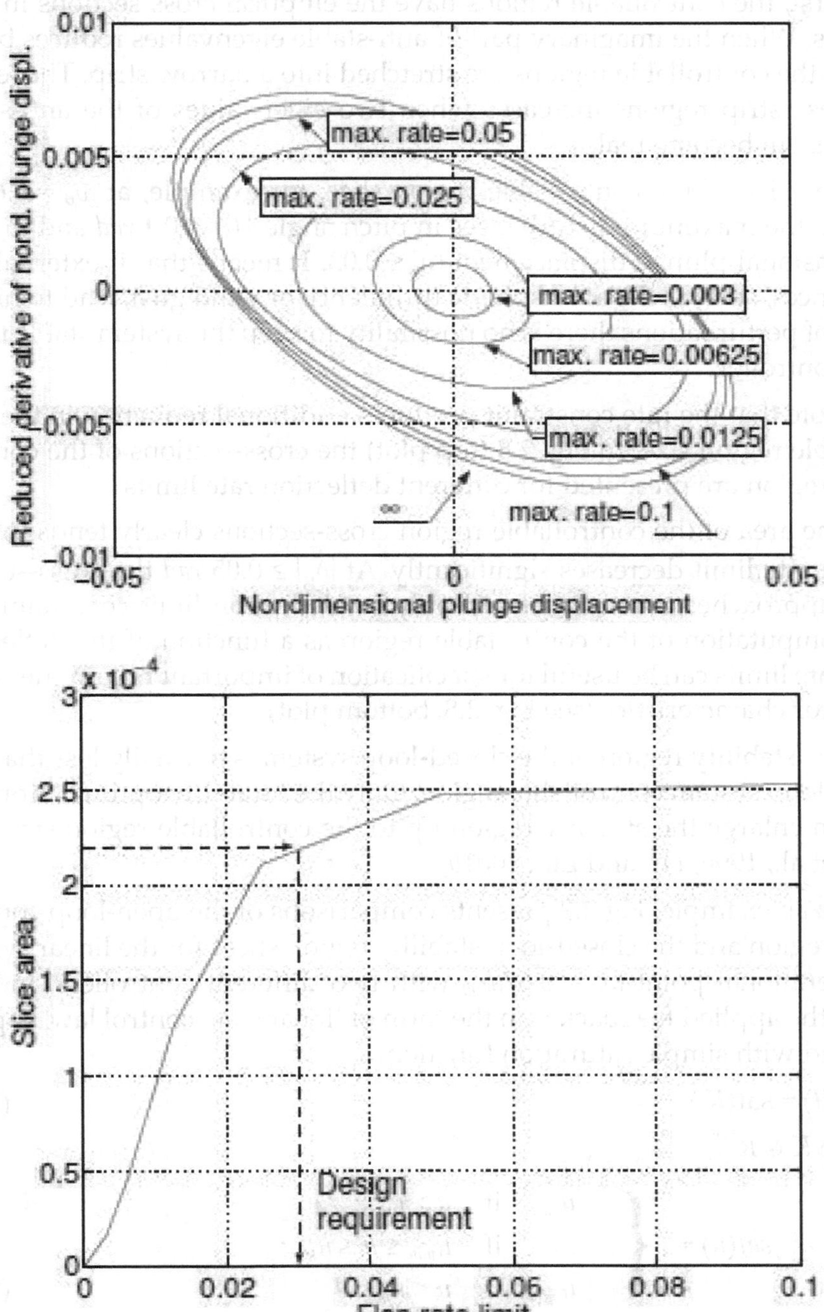

Figure 2.8: Controllable region slices at $\omega\theta = 0.67\omega_{\theta fl}$ for different rate limits (top plot) and the area of these slices versus the rate limit (bottom plot). The deflection limit $|\delta c| \leq 0.1$ *rad*.

First, the controllable regions have the elliptical cross-sections in both planes. When the imaginary part of anti-stable eigenvalues reduces below ≈ 0.08 the controllable regions are stretched into a narrow strip. The length of these strip regions increases when two eigenvalues of the anti-stable subsystem become real.

The size of the controllable region slice, for example, at $\omega_\theta = 0.67\omega_{\theta fl}$ allows the maximum disturbances in pitch angle $|\theta| \leq 0.1$ *rad* and in non-dimensional plunge displacement $|\bar{h}| \leq 0.03$. It means that if external disturbances, such as the atmospheric turbulence or wind gust, lead to higher level of perturbations there is no possibility to keep the system stable using any controller.

Note that the rate constraint produces additional reduction in the controllable region size. In Fig. 2.8 (top plot) the cross-sections of the controllable region are presented for different deflection rate limits.

The area of the controllable region cross-sections clearly tends to zero as the rate limit decreases significantly. At $|\dot{\delta}_c| \geq 0.05$ *rad* the cross-section area approaches the size defined only by deflection limit constraints. So the computation of the controllable region as a function of the deflection and rate limits can be useful for specification of important requirements for actuator characteristics (see Fig. 2.8, bottom plot).

The stability region of the closed-loop system is normally less than the open-loop system controllable region. Only the "stability optimal" controller can enlarge the stability region up to the controllable region size (Goman et al., 1996; Hu and Lin, 2001*b*).

As an example, Fig.2.9 presents comparisons of the open-loop controllable region and the closed-loop stability region slices for the linear system at operational point $\omega_\theta = 0.67\omega_{\theta fl}$ with two different controllers. In both cases the applied feedback is in the form of linear state control law, supplemented with simple saturation function:

$$\delta_c(t) = \text{sat}(K_x) \tag{2.34}$$

where $K \in R^{1\times n}$,

$$sat(u) = \begin{cases} u_{max}, & \text{if} \quad u > u_{max}; \\ u, & \text{if} \quad u_{min} \leq u \leq u_{max}; \\ u_{min}, & \text{if} \quad u < u_{min}; \end{cases} \tag{2.35}$$

and $u_{max} = -u_{min} = 0.1$ *rad*.

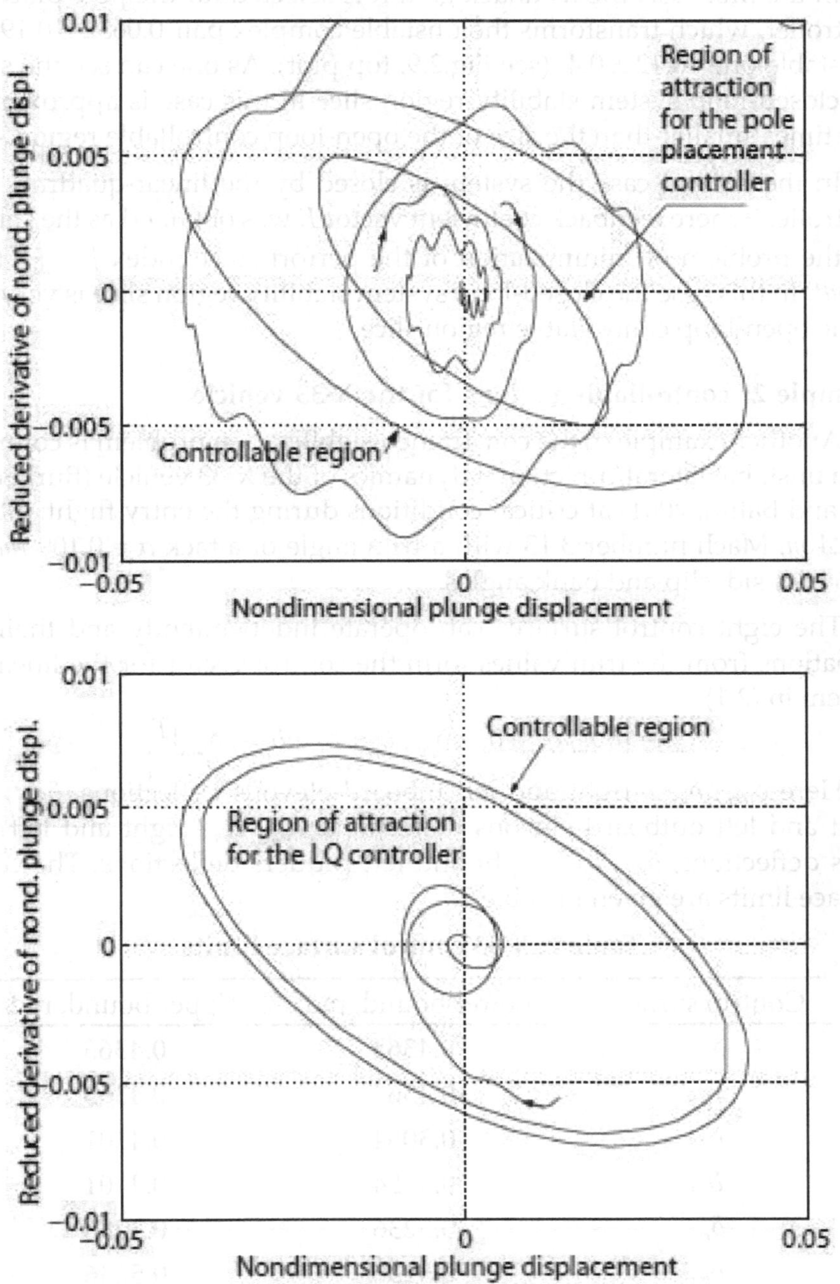

Figure 2.9: Comparison of the controllable region at $\omega_\theta = 0.67\omega_{\theta fl}$ with the regions of attraction for the closed-loop system: slices for the pole placement controller (top plot) and for the linear-quadratic controller (bottom plot). The deflection limit $|\delta_c| \leq 0.1$ *rad*.

In the first case, the feedback gain K is selected for the pole placement controller, which transforms the unstable complex pair $0.0632 \pm 0.1994i$ to the stable one $-0.12 \pm 0.4i$ (see Fig.2.9, top plot). As one can see the size of the closed-loop system stability region slice in this case is approximately two times smaller than the size of the open-loop controllable region slice.

In the second case the system is closed by the linear-quadratic (LQ) controller, where feedback coefficient vector K was obtained as the solution for the problem of minimization of the performance index $J = \int_0^\infty (x^T x + u^T u)dt$. In this case the closed-loop system stability region slice is very close to the open-loop controllable region slice.

Example 2: controllable regions for the X-33 vehicle

Another example of the constrained stabilization problem is connected with unstable lateral/directional dynamics of the X-33 vehicle (Burken, Lu, Wu and Bahm, 2001) at critical conditions during the entry flight: altitude 29624 *m*, Mach number 3.13 with a trim angle of attack $\alpha = 0.109$ *rad* and zero trim sideslip and bank angles.

The eight control surfaces can operate independently and their perturbations from the trim values form the control vector for the linearized system in (2.1):

$$u = [\delta_{revi}, \delta_{levi}, \delta_{rbf}, \delta_{lbf}, \delta_{rvr}, \delta_{lvr}, \delta_{revo}, \delta_{levo}]^T.$$

Here δ_{revi}, δ_{levi} - right and left inboard elevons deflections, δ_{revo}, δ_{levo} - right and left outboard elevons deflections, δ_{rbf}, δ_{lbf} - right and left body flaps deflections, δ_{rvr}, δ_{lvr} - right and left rudders deflections. The control sufrace limits are given in Table 2.

Table 2. X-33 control surface limits

Control surface	Lower bound, rad	Upper bound, rad
δ_{revi}	-0.4363	0.4363
δ_{levi}	-0.4363	0.4363
δ_{rbf}	-0.3054	0.4101
δ_{lbf}	-0.3054	0.4101
δ_{rvr}	-0.5236	0.5236
δ_{lvr}	-0.5236	0.5236
δ_{revo}	-0.4363	0.4363
δ_{levo}	-0.4363	0.4363

The state vector in the system defined by (2.1) combines the longitudinal and lat-eral/directional motion parameters:

$$x = [P, R, \beta, \phi, \psi, \alpha, Q, \theta, V]^T.$$

Here P, Q, R - the roll, pitch and yaw rates, α, β - the angle of attack and sideslip angle, ϕ, ψ - the bank and heading angles, V - the aircraft velocity.

The matrices of the linearized X-33 vehicle for the above flight conditions are given in (Burken et al., 2001):

$$A = 10^{-3} \times \begin{bmatrix} A_{lat} & 0 \\ 0 & A_{lon} \end{bmatrix}$$

with

$$A_{lat} = \begin{bmatrix} -96.95 & 28.11 & 673.08 & 0 & 0 \\ 4.42 & -34.78 & -936.95 & 0 & 0 \\ -0.019 & -999.94 & -36.18 & 10.27 & -0.95 \\ 1000 & 0 & 0 & 0 & 0 \\ 0 & 1000 & 0 & 0 & 0 \end{bmatrix}$$

$$A_{lon} = \begin{bmatrix} -70.55 & 1000.3 & 0.954 & 0.038 \\ -1546.3 & -52.24 & 0 & -0.046 \\ 0 & 1000 & 0 & 0 \\ -550.04 & 0 & -559.09 & -13.375 \end{bmatrix}$$

and

$$B = \begin{bmatrix} -0.2137 & 0.2137 & -0.8418 & 0.8418 & 0.0115 & \dots \\ 0.0448 & -0.0448 & 0.3639 & -0.3639 & -0.0077 & \dots \\ -0.0001 & 0.0001 & 0.0003 & -0.0003 & 0 & \dots \\ 0 & 0 & 0 & 0 & 0 & \dots \\ 0 & 0 & 0 & 0 & 0 & \dots \\ -0.0003 & -0.0003 & -0.0017 & -0.0017 & 0.000004 & \dots \\ -0.0617 & -0.0617 & -0.5393 & -0.5393 & 0.005 & \dots \\ 0 & 0 & 0 & 0 & 0 & \dots \\ -0.0034 & -0.0034 & -0.1285 & -0.1285 & 0.0011 & \dots \end{bmatrix}$$

$$\left.\begin{matrix}
0.0115 & -0.2612 & 0.2621 \\
-0.0077 & 0.0548 & -0.0548 \\
0 & -0.0002 & 0.0002 \\
0 & 0 & 0 \\
0 & 0 & 0 \\
-0.000004 & -0.0004 & 0.0004 \\
-0.005 & -0.0754 & 0.0754 \\
0 & 0 & 0 \\
-0.0011 & -0.0041 & -0.0041
\end{matrix}\right]$$

Table 3 shows the open-loop poles. Note that the first five eigenvalues represent the lateral/directional dynamics and the last four eigenvalues represent the longitudinal dynamics.

Although the linearized longitudinal and lateral/directional motions are decoupled in the matrix A, all control surfaces in different extent contribute both to longitudinal and lateral/directional dynamics. Hence the control law design must be carried out simultaneously for longitudinal and lateral modes. (Burken et al., 2001) There are two anti-stable eigenvalues in the system, the most significant λ_2 is produced due to directional aerodynamic instability, and the second one λ_9 is very slow phugoid mode instability in the longitudinal motion. The controllable region slices in the planes (β, P) and (R, P) of the lateral/directional parameters have the form of a strip (see Fig. 2.10, 2.11, 2.12).

The controllable region cross-sections have been first computed without account of the rate constraints. And the two stabilizing control laws, the LQ optimal controller (designed in the same manner as for the aeroservoelastic problem in the previous section) and the pole placement controller, have been compared in terms of slices of their closed-loop stability regions.

To take into account control constraints, the saturation function given in (2.35) was implemented for each control input. The slice of the domain of attraction for the LQ optimal controller covers a large part of the controllable region slice, as shown in Fig. 2.10. In Fig. 2.11 the cross-sections of the closed-loop system stability region are shown for the pole placement controller. The closed-loop system eigenvalues in this case have been assigned as shown in Table 3. Note that during control synthesis only body flaps have been considered as active.

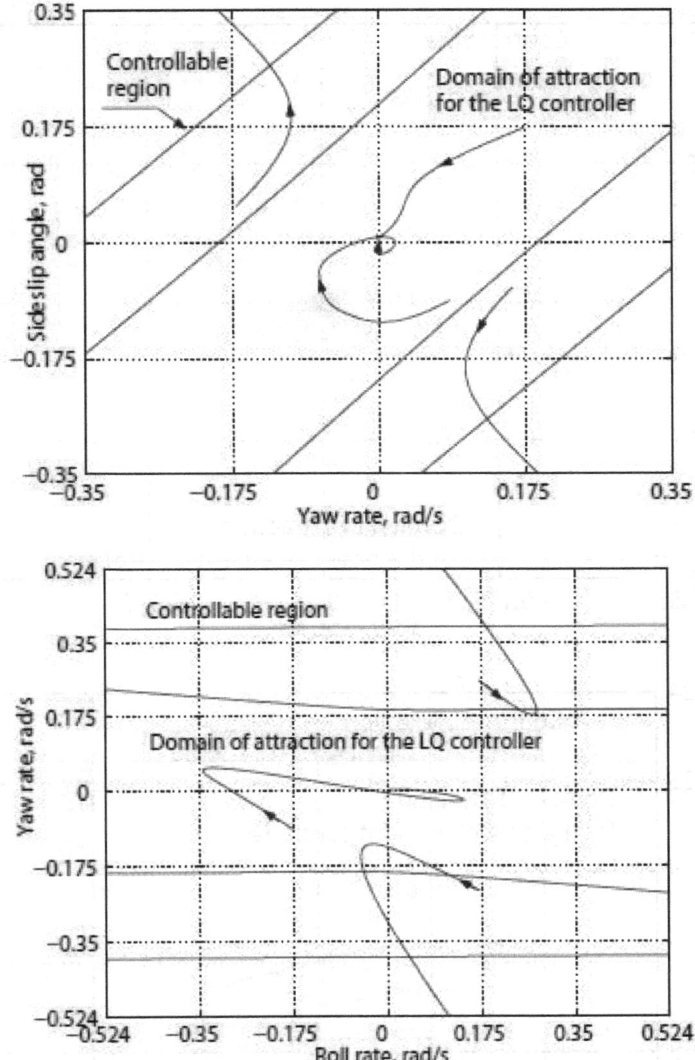

Figure 2.10: X-33 linearized model. Comparison of controllable and stability region cross-sections at the presence of only deflection constraints: the linear-quadratic controller.

The results presented demonstrate that in the both cases the closed-loop system stability regions are less than the controllable region. The pole placement control law can produce an unsatisfactory size for the stability region for the closed-loop system when the assigned locations of the closed-loop eigenvalues are taken without consideration of the stability region size.

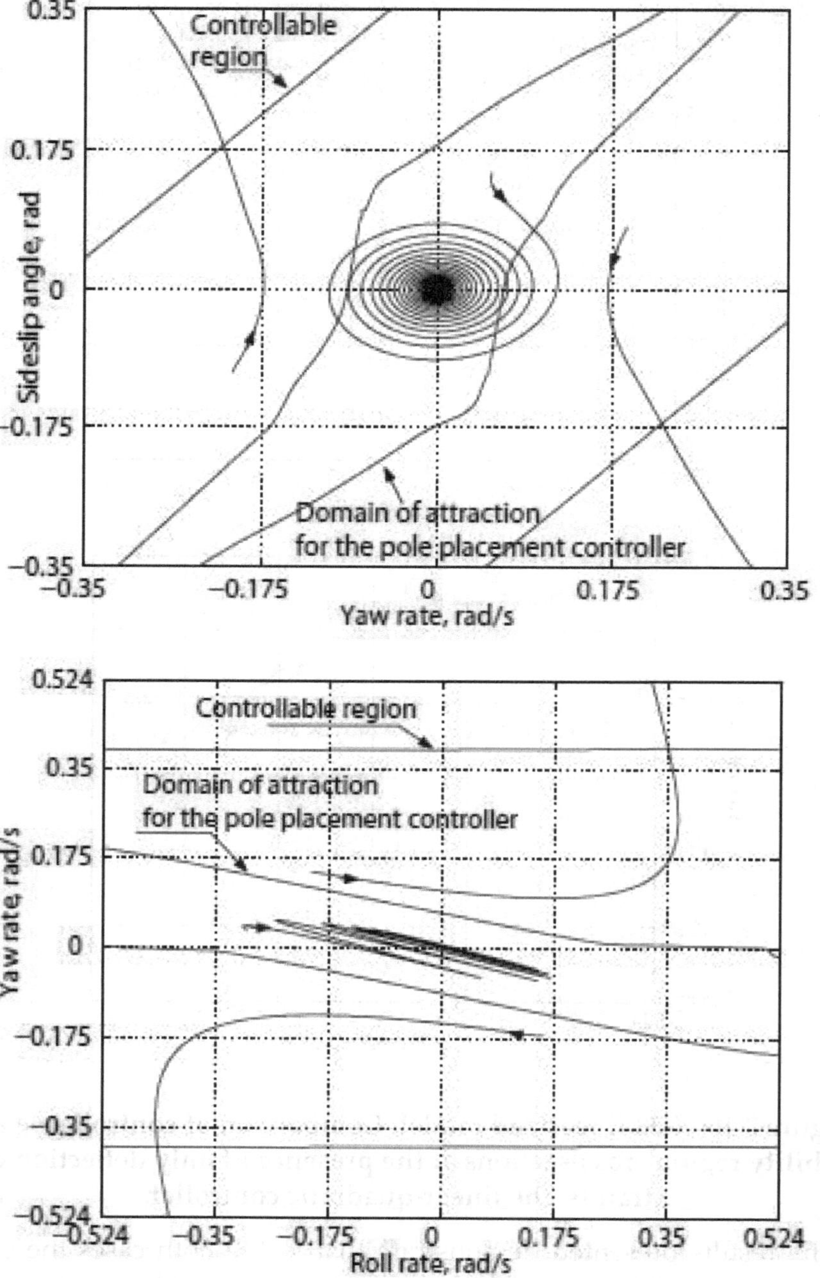

Figure 2.11: X-33 linearized model. Comparison of controllable and stability region cross-sections at the presence of only deflection constraints: the pole placement controller.

Table 3. Eigenvalues of the X-33 model

	Open-loop	Closed-loop
$\lambda_1 =$	-1.0007	-0.4 + 1.25i
$\lambda_2 =$	0.93495	-0.4 - 1.25i
$\lambda_3 =$	-0.102	-0.102
$\lambda_4 =$	-0.000562	-0.0562
$\lambda_5 =$	0	-0.01
$\lambda_6 =$	-0.0609 + 1.24i	-0.0609 + 1.24i
$\lambda_7 =$	-0.0609 - 1.24i	-0.0609 - 1.24i
$\lambda_8 =$	-0.0149	-0.0149
$\lambda_9 =$	0.000646	-0.0646

To demonstrate the rate limit influence on the controllable region size the absolute values of rates for all control effectors have been limited by the same value. The cross-sections of the controllable region in the planes (β, P) and (R, P) for maximum rate limit 0.35 and 0.175 *rad/s* are shown in Fig. 2.12. One can see that even these very slow actuators are not very critical in terms of the size of the controllable region, since the decrease of the controllable region slice due to rate saturation in this case is relatively small.

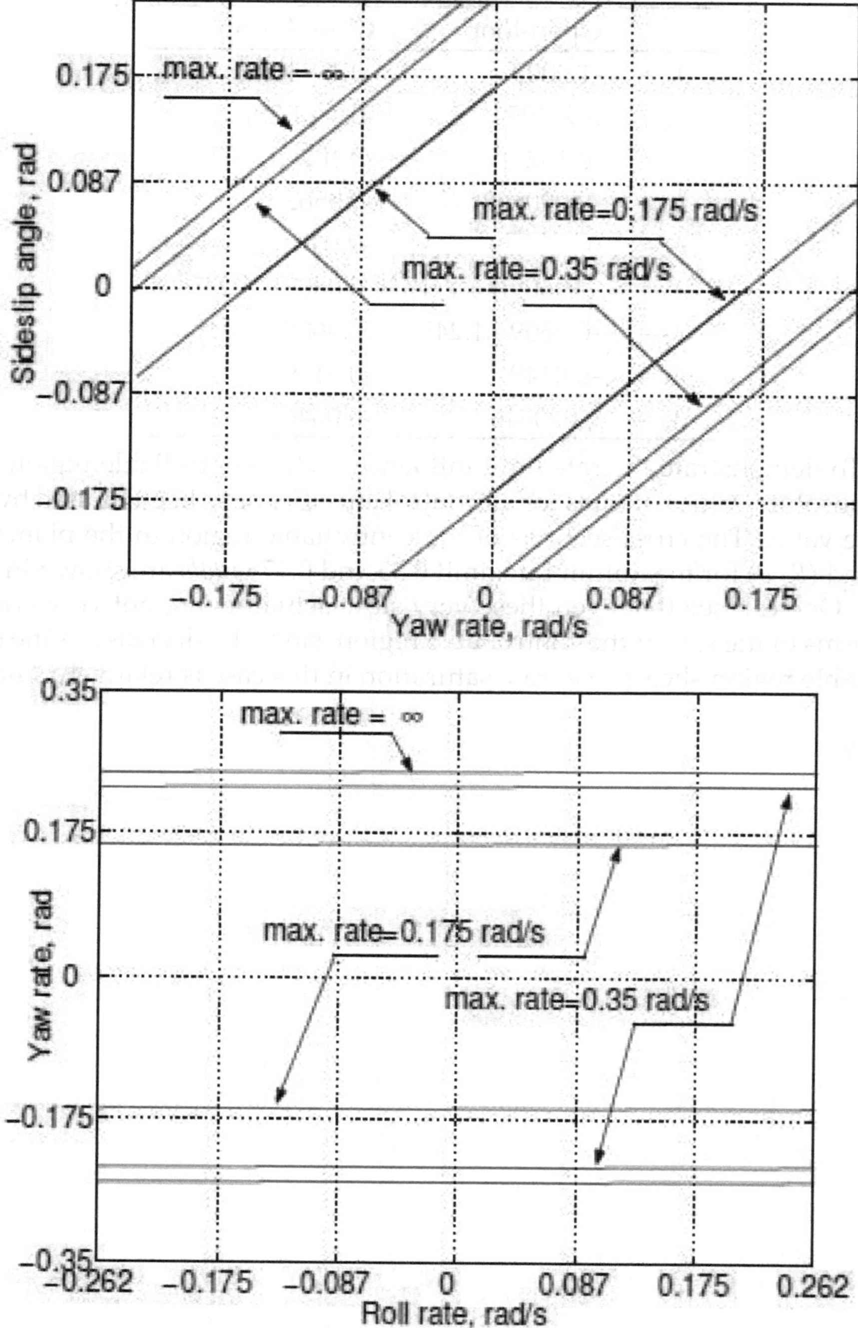

Figure 2.12: X-33 linearized model. Comparison of controllable region cross-sections for different rate limits.

2.5 Conclusion

The proposed numerical algorithm for the computation of the controllable regions for unstable linear systems with two types of control constraints such as deflection limit and rate saturation can be applied for post design assessment of different control laws and specification of design requirements for actuator characteristics. This method allows an unlimited number of control effectors and anti-stable eigenvalues in the open-loop system. The computational examples presented for the simple aeroservoelastic system and the aerodynamically unstable X-33 vehicle demonstrate the utility of the proposed method for design and post-design assessment of control laws at flight regimes with unstable dynamics.

Chapter 3

Maximization of Stability Region

In this chapter the problem of linear controller design maximizing the closed-loop system stability region is considered for the linearized system with one and two unstable eigenvalues and only deflection constraints. The results presented in (Goman et al., 1996) are extended to the case of multiple control inputs considering two flight control design examples. The proposed control design method can be expressed in terms of linear matrix inequalities (LMI) and therefore can be combined with other performance conditions imposed via LMI, thus providing us with a tool for control law design combining stability and performance characteristics.

3.1 Previous developments in the field

In an intrinsically unstable system, control saturation can lead to significant degradation of dynamic characteristics or even to the loss of stability in the closed-loop system. As we have learned from the previous chapter, an unstable constrained linear system has a bounded controllable region, where the stabilization problem can be solved. In many practical situations associated with a high level of instability and low control authority, the controllable region decreases significantly and classical linear control design methods lose their efficiency. Then the engineer needs to perform extensive simulations and subsequent tuning of the control law parameters. It makes sense then to develop control methods that can take into account the stability region size on a regular basis.

The number of papers considering maximization of the stability region is growing, fol-lowing the recent trend of tremendous activity in the area of control synthesis for systems with state and control constraints. For linear, input constrained systems this methodology is now rather well developed.

The best controller in terms of the stability region size has to keep the system stable in the whole controllable region. Such a controller is called the "maximum stabilizer" (Scibile and Kouvaritakis, 2000) or "stability optimal" one (Grishanin, Lebedev, Lipatov and Stepanjantz, 1999; Goman et al., 1996). The controller of some particular structure designed with additional criteria for maximizing the stability region (Kamenetskiy, 1996; Pare, Hindi, How and Boyd, 1998; Henrion, Tarbouriech and Kuˇcera, 2001) can be called a "stability suboptimal" one. The question of how to determine a stabilizing regulator that would yield the largest domain of attraction for an unstable plant with control bounds was posed first in (Stepanjantz, 1985).

Regarding practical applications, the problem was addressed in the context of tokamak control (Scibile, 1997; Scibile and Kouvaritakis, 2000), unstable aircraft stabilization (Glad, 1996; Goman et al., 1996; Barbu, Galeani, Teel and Zaccarian, 2005) and flutter suppression (Goman and Demenkov, 2004*a*; Applebaum and Ben-Asher, 2007).

The contributions to the problem of stability region maximization are of two different kinds.

3.1.1 Maximum stabilizer design

The first kind deals with the absolute optimal or near optimal solutions, i.e. conversion of the controllable region or its high-accuracy approximation into a stability region of the closed-loop system.

The simplest case of one unstable eigenvalue and amplitude control constraints has been considered for example in (Glad, 1995; Scibile and Kouvaritakis, 2000). The resulting optimal controller is of the bang-bang type that switches about the hyperplane obtained from the corresponding eigenvector.

From Gamkrelidze's theorem (Pontryagin et al., 1962) the time-optimal control law has a conversion property (Scibile, 1997) and therefore the solution can be obtained via the Pontryagin's minimum principle.

The basic version of the minimum principle can cope only with amplitude control con-straints and requires the solution of a two-point boundary value problem. The advanced version can cope even with the amplitude constraints on the input and state variables constraints, thus it can address both the amplitude and rate constraints on the input.

A simple solution to the problem (Grishanin et al., 1999) has been proposed using the minimum principle for the case of one unstable eigenvalue. It takes into account both amplitude and rate control constraints. However, for an increased number of unstable poles, due to the limitations of the computational resources available, it is still not possible to implement such a solution in real-time applications. Nevertheless, these results point out to nonlinear control laws as the more efficient way of problem solution than the linear ones.

The approach for two-dimensional single-input continuous systems with amplitude con-straints $|u| \le u_{max}$ has been proposed in (Goman et al., 1996), where the optimal control law is the relay-type ($u(t) = \pm u_{max}$) and specified by a switching line. Two equilibrium points $\pm A^{-1}Bu_{max}$ are positioned on this line, which is derived using geometric nonlinear dynamic analysis (see Fig. 3.1). The stability region in this case is bounded by the limit cycle curves. The optimal solution also induces a set of suboptimal linear control laws, for which each row vector in their gain matrices is orthogonal to the optimal switching line. For higher order systems, the solution can be found for the unstable subspace of state-space with no more than two dimensions.

In (Hu and Lin, 2001*b*) it was established that for single-input linear systems having two exponentially unstable poles, the LQ-optimal controller provides the (full observable) system with a domain of attraction, which approaches the controllable region as the loop gain is increased towards infinity. It is interesting to note that in this case the relay-type "stability optimal" control law tends to be exactly the same as the controller proposed in (Goman et al., 1996).

Let P be the unique positive definite solution to the following algebraic Riccati equation:

$$A^T P + PA - P^T BB^T P = 0$$

Note that this equation is associated with the minimum energy regulation, i.e., an LQR problem with cost $J = \int_0^\infty u^T(t)u(t)dt$. The corresponding minimum energy state feedback gain is given by

$$K = -B^T P.$$

A linear system (without constraints) under LQ control has the following properties (Hu and Lin, 2001*b*):

- The loop gain can be increased indefinitely without loss of stability.
- The loop gain can be halved and stability will still be maintained.

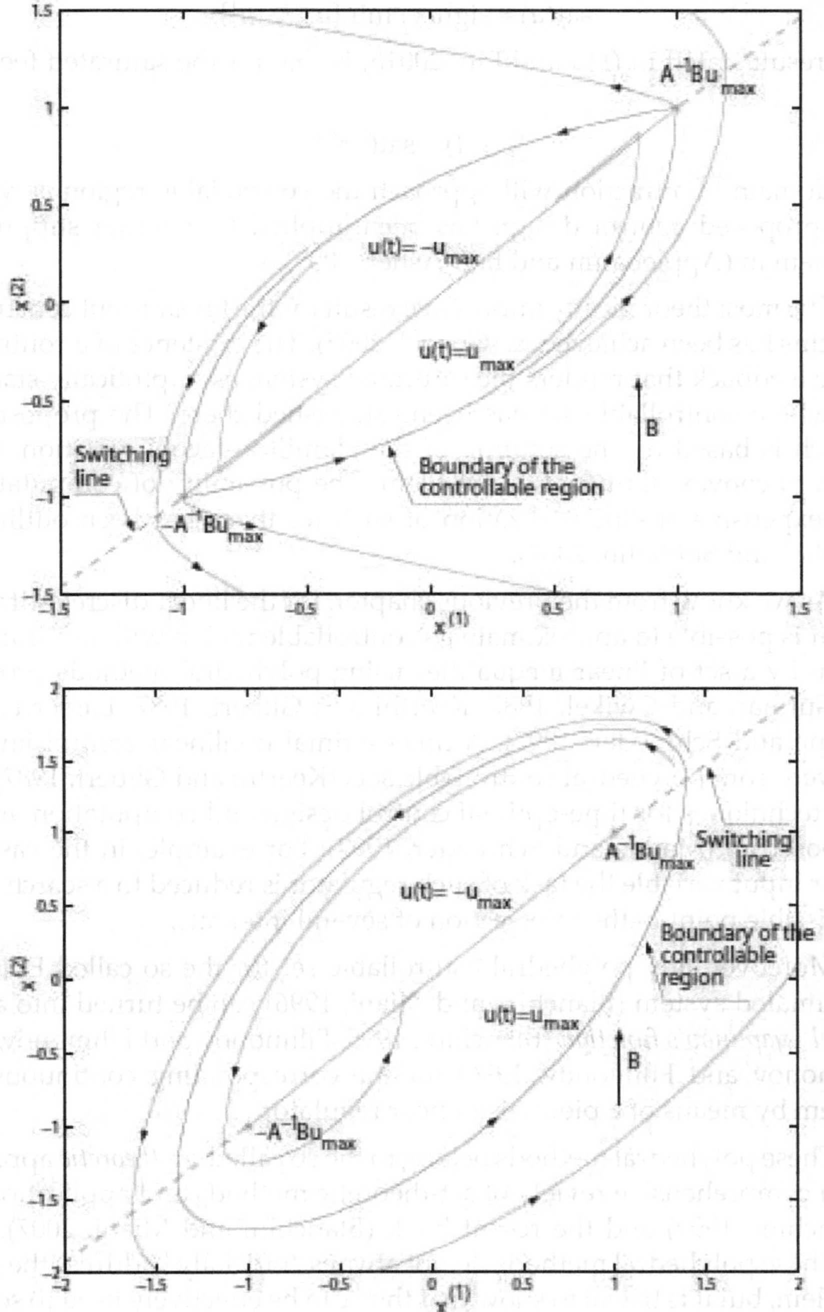

Figure 3.1: Stability optimal relay control law: a system with two real eigenvalues (top plot) and with two complex eigenvalues (bottom plot).

Consider the standard saturation function

$$\text{sat}(u) = \text{sign}(u)\min\{u_{max},\ |u|\}.$$

The result stated in (Hu and Lin, 2001*b*) is that for the saturated feedback law

$$u(t) = \text{sat}(\gamma K_x)$$

the domain of attraction will approach the controllable region as $\gamma \to \infty$. The proposed control design has been applied to a flutter suppression problem in (Applebaum and Ben-Asher, 2007).

The most theoretically impressive result for the linear input constrained systems has been achieved in (Goebel, 2005). The existence of a continuous static feedback that renders the saturated system asymptotically stable on the whole controllable set has been established there. The proposed approach is based on the solution of the Hamilton-Jacobi equation, which leads to convex optimization problem. The possibility of computationally inexpensive on-line realization of such feedback has been outlined in (Goebel and Subbotin, 2007).

As we know from the previous chapter, for the linear discrete-time system it is possible to approximate its controllable region with arbitrary precision by a set of linear inequalities using polyhedral methods proposed in (Gutman and Cwikel, 1987; Keerthi and Gilbert, 1987; Lasserre, 1993; Mayne and Schroeder, 1997). A time-optimal nonlinear control law was derived from polyhedral controllable sets (Keerthi and Gilbert, 1987). Various techniques for time-optimal control design and computation are also proposed in (Mayne and Schroeder, 1997). For example, in the case of a scalar input variable the task of such regulator is reduced to a search for an admissible point in the intersection of several intervals.

Moreover, any polyhedral controllable set for the so called Euler approximated system (Blanchini and Miani, 1996) can be turned into a *polyhedral Lyapunov's function* (Blanchini, 1995; Filimonov and Filimonov, 1995; Filimonov and Filimonov, 1996) for the corresponding continuous-time system by means of a piecewise-linear regulator.

These polyhedral methods belong to the so called *set-theoretic* approach. For a comprehensive review of set-theoretic methods and applications see (Blanchini, 1999) and the recent book (Blanchini and Miani, 2007). Note that these polyhedral methods do not always "officially" address the posed problem, but it is trivial to show that they can be effectively used to solve it.

3.1.2 Parametric design

The second kind of contributions deals with the problem of parametric optimization. This problem consists in assigning the regulator parameters so that the stability region becomes in some sense optimal in size, while the regulator has a specified structure.

Parametric design procedures, which are based on Lyapunov's function method, has been proposed first in (Kamenetskiy, 1996), by means of stability analysis techniques from (Kamenetskiy, 1995), all applied to continuous nonlinear systems. The considered class of closed-loop systems is restricted to those having two-time differentiable right-hand side in the state-space form, with a predefined number of regulator parameters. Hence, in the case of control constraints they must be defined via differentiable functions. The proposed methods consist in modifying the Lyapunov's function via its parameters simultaneously with the regulator parameters along solution curves of special differential inclusion. The state-space variables of that inclusion are the parameter vector that consists both of the Lyapunov's function and regulator parameters. There is no system order restriction. The stability regions are bounded by a level surface of the Lyapunov's function. There are three proposed optimization criteria: the first is an augmentation of the stability region in the sense of the level surface of the Lyapunov's function, the second is an augmentation in the sense of inclusion and the third is an augmentation along some prespecified directions in the state-space, which are of expert choice.

Various techniques for parametric LMI-based optimization, performed to enlarge the stability region, are discussed in (Pare et al., 1998; Henrion, Tarbouriech and Garcia, 1999; Henrion and Tarbouriech, 1999; Henrion et al., 2001).

An approach that is also based on quadratic Lyapunov functions and LMI formulations is discussed in the book(Hu and Lin, 2001*b*) along with the methods already outlined above. Since this book has been completely dedicated to the study of controllable region properties and stability optimal regulator design, it is a highly recommended reading for anyone who wants to understand the field. The book's contents have been described also in numerous journal publications (Hu and Lin, 2000; Hu, Lin and Qiu, 2001; Hu and Lin, 2001*a*; Hu and Lin, 2001*c*; Lin and Hu, 2001; Hu, Lin and Shamash, 2001; Hu, Lin and Chen, 2002*a*; Hu and Lin, 2002*a*; Hu and Lin, 2002*b*; Cao, Lin and Hu, 2002; Hu, Lin and Chen, 2002*b*). This research has been continued using the combinations of several quadratic functions in (Hu and Lin, 2003; Hu, Goebel, Teel and Lin, 2005).

Another interesting branch of research is connected with the determination of stability regions for linear systems with saturating controls through *anti-windup* schemes.

Suppose that a linear feedback $u_c(t)$ has been designed to stabilize the linear system without saturation. In order to mitigate the undesirable effects of windup caused by input saturation, an anti-windup term E can be added to the controller:

$$u\square(t) = A_c u(t) + B_c x(t) + E(\text{sat}(u_c(t)) - u_c(t)).$$

Several LMI-based methods have been proposed (Cao, Lin and Ward, 2002; Cao, Lin and Ward, 2004; Tarbouriech, da Silva and Garcia, 2003; da Silva and Tarbouriech, 2005; da Silva and Tarbouriech, 2006; Tarbouriech, Queinnec and Garcia, 2006) for designing an anti-windup gain E that maximizes an estimate of the basin of attraction of the closed-loop system in the presence of saturation.

Another approach to the problem is to synthesize an antiwindup compensator that works as an add-on for any a priori given controller outside its region of linearity (Barbu et al., 2005; Avanzini and Galeani, 2005; Galeani, Teel and Zaccarian, 2007). The boundaries of the stability region in the system state space are then independent of the unconstrained controller dynamics and are only dependent on the structural limitations of the saturated system.

It is obvious that one can compute the stability region using a grid of points. However,this approach can be very time consuming. To compute reasonable estimations of stability regions, various techniques have been proposed in the literature, based on Lyapunov's function method (Kametnetskiy, 1995; Peterfreund and Baram, 1998; da Silva and Tarbouriech, 1999; Julian, Guivant and Desages, 1999; Turner and Postlethwaite, 2001).

3.2 Problem statement

It is supposed that the following continuous time-invariant linear system:

$$\square(t) = Ax(t) + Bu(t) \tag{3.1}$$

with $A \in R^{n\times n}$, $B \in R^{n\times m}$, $x \in R^n$, $u \in R^m$ has $q \le n$ anti-stable eigenvalues λ_i, $Re\lambda_i > 0$, $i = 1, \ldots, q$ and the control vector is bounded:

$$u \in U, \tag{3.2}$$

where $U \in Rm$ is a compact and convex set, which is defined in the form of amplitude constraints:

$$|u^{(i)}| \le u^{(i)}_{max}, i = \overline{1,m}. \tag{3.3}$$

It is additionally supposed that the matrix A has no neutral eigenvalues and the state vector is fully observable.

Considering the problem of system stabilization and maximization of the closed-loop system stability region, below only the subspace corresponding to unstable eigenvalues will be considered.

The dynamics associated with the anti-stable eigenvalues is described by the following reduced-order subsystem (see Chapter 2):

$$\dot{z}(t) = A_z z(t) + B_z u(t), \tag{3.4}$$

where $A_z \in R^{q\times q}$, $B_z \in R^{q\times m}$, $u(t) \in U$ and $z(t) = Q^T_2\, x(t)$.

If system (3.4) is stabilized and its states approach equilibrium point with $z(t) = 0$ and $u(t) = 0$, it is trivial to show that the stable subsystem $s(t)$ will also asymptotically approach the origin and thus to stabilize system (3.1) it is enough to stabilize only subsystem $z(t)$ (3.4). The bounded controllable region C of the anti-stable subsystem produces a cylinder in the full state-space of original system, which is unbounded in some directions.

Suppose that system (3.1) is stabilized by the linear controller:

$$u(t) = Kx(t), \tag{3.5}$$

where $K \in R^{mxn}$ stabilizes the closed-loop system (3.1), (3.5) in the absence of control saturation.

To take into account control constraints, consider the saturation function defined for scalar $u^{(i)} \in R^1$ as:

$$\text{sat}(u^{(i)}) = \begin{cases} u^{(i)}_{max}; & u^{(i)} > u^{(i)}_{max} \\ u^{(i)}; & |u^{(i)}| \le u^{(i)}_{max} \\ -u^{(i)}_{max}; & u^{(i)} < -u^{(i)}_{max} \end{cases}$$

and for vector $u = [u^{(1)}, \ldots, u^{(m)}]^T$ as:

$$\text{sat}(u) = [\text{sat}(u^{(1)}), \ldots, \text{sat}(u^{(m)})]^T.$$

The constrained linear closed-loop system is defined by (3.1) and the following nonlinear control:

$$u(t) = \text{sat}(Kx(t)). \tag{3.6}$$

We will operate with the following definition of the *stability* region.

Definition 4 *The stability region S of system (3.1) closed by feedback control (3.6) is the set of all points $x_0 \in R^n$ from which the closed-loop system asymptotically approaches the origin:*

$$S = \{x_0 \in R^n : \lim_{t\to\infty} x^{(i)}(t, x_0) = 0, \forall i = \overline{1, n}\}.$$

The optimal stability region S_{opt} is equal to the controllable region C.

In this chapter the computation of the controllable region C and the linear controller design maximizing the stability region S of the constrained closed-loop system is considered for cases, when matrix A has one or two unstable eigenvalues and system (3.1) has multiple control inputs $m \geq 1$.

3.3 Maximum stabilizer design for one-dimensional case

The anti-stable subsystem is described by the first-order differential equation:

$$\dot{z}(t) = a_z z(t) + b_z u(t),$$

where $a_z > 0$, $b_z \in R^{1\times m}$, $u(t) \in U$ and $z(t) = Q^T_2\, x(t)$.

The closed-loop system is stable if the following algebraic stability conditions hold:

$$z > 0 \Rightarrow \dot{z} < 0;$$
$$z = 0 \Rightarrow \dot{z} = 0;$$
$$z < 0 \Rightarrow \dot{z} > 0.$$

Consider the upper limit on z, while $\dot{z} < 0$:

$$z < \frac{1}{a_z}(-\sum_{i=1}^{m} b_z^{(i)} u^{(i)}) \leq \max_{u\in U} \frac{1}{a_z}(-\sum_{i=1}^{m} b_z^{(i)} u^{(i)}) = \frac{1}{a_z}\sum_{i=1}^{m} b_z^{(i)} u_{max}^{(i)} \mathrm{sign}(b_z^{(i)}).$$

Applying the same reasoning to obtain the lower limit on z, while $\dot{z} > 0$, one can see that the controllable region of the unstable subsystem is an interval: $-z_{max} < z < z_{max}$,

where

$$z_{max} = \frac{1}{a_z}(\sum_{i=1}^{m} |b_z^{(i)}| u_{max}^{(i)}). \tag{3.7}$$

In the state-space of the original system the controllable region looks like a "strip" that is defined by the following linear inequality:

$$-z_{max} < Q^T_2 x < z_{max}. \tag{3.8}$$

To derive a saturated linear control law $u^{(i)}(t) = \mathrm{sat}(k_i z(t))$ maximizing the closed-loop system stability region it is necessary to satisfy the following two requirements:

1. In the absence of saturation the closed-loop system must be stable

$$a_z + \sum_{i=1}^{m} b_z^{(i)} k_i < 0; \tag{3.9}$$

2. On the boundary of controllable region the saturated control must satisfy the special conditions, which minimize $\dot{z}$ if $z > 0$ and maximize $\dot{z}$ if $z < 0$. They result in the following inequalities for each k_i:

$$b^{(i)} < 0 \Rightarrow k_i z_{max} \geq u_{max}^{(i)}$$

$$b^{(i)} > 0 \Rightarrow k_i z_{max} \leq -u_{max}^{(i)}$$

$$b^{(i)} = 0 \Rightarrow k_i = 0 \tag{3.10}$$

Any linear control law that satisfies the system of linear inequalities (3.9) and (3.10) is the maximum stabilizer, i.e. it provides the system with the maximal stability region, which is equal to controllable region C. This control law can be computed, for example, via linear programming.

To illustrate the method, let us consider the following linearized lateral-directional dynamics of an aircraft without a vertical tail (Ngo, Reigelsperger, Banda and Bessolo, 1996). The stability and controllability matrices correspond to flight at Mach number $M = 0.4$, altitude $H = 15000$ ft and angle of attack $\alpha = 8.8$ deg:

$$[A|B] = \left[\begin{array}{ccc|ccccc} -0.004 & 0.154 & -0.988 & -0.009 & 0.013 & 0.006 & 0.011 & -0.004 \\ -8.21 & -0.785 & 0.117 & 7.57 & -4.97 & 3.65 & 0.079 & -0.614 \\ -0.889 & -0.03 & -0.016 & 0.091 & -0.181 & -0.416 & -0.804 & 0.188 \end{array}\right].$$

The state vector $x = [\beta, p, r]^T$, where β is the sideslip angle in degrees, p, r are the body-axis roll and yaw rates in degrees per second. The control vector $u = [\delta_e, \delta_s, \delta_t, \delta_{ytv}, \delta_f]^T$, where δ_e is the differential elevons, δ_s is the differential spoiler/slot-deflectors, δ_t is the differential all moving tips, δ_{ytv} is the yaw thrust vectoring, and δ_f is the differential outboard leading-edge flaps, all control deflections are expressed in degrees.

The following unstable subsystem can be obtained via the Schur decomposition of matrix A:

$$[a_z|b_z] = \left[\begin{array}{c|ccccc} 0.434 & -0.485 & 0.206 & -0.654 & -0.737 & 0.218 \end{array}\right].$$

The variable z of unstable subspace is connected with the system state vector x as

$$z(t) = Q_2^T x(t), \quad Q_2^T = [\ -0.421 \quad -0.075 \quad 0.904\ ].$$

All control variables are constrained by the same value: $|u^{(i)}| \le 5\ deg$, $i = \overline{1,5}$ In accordance with (3.7) and (3.8) the controllable region of unstable subsystem is defined by $z_{max} = 26.472$.

To compute the maximum stabilizer the following system of linear inequalities must be solved:

$$0.434 - 0.485k_1 + 0.206k_2 - 0.654k_3 - 0.737k_4 + 0.218k_5 \le \gamma,$$

$$26.472k_1 \ge 5,\ 26.472k_2 \le -5,\ 26.472k_3 \ge 5,\ 26.472k_4 \ge 5,\ 26.472k_5 \le -5,$$

where $\gamma < 0$.

One of the possible solutions for $\gamma = -1$ is

$$k_1 = 0.5365,\ k_2 = -0.2276,\ k_3 = 0.7236,\ k_4 = 0.816,\ k_5 = -0.2412.$$

The final step is to convert the control law to a linear function of the original system state vector:

$$K_{max} = \begin{bmatrix} k_1 Q_2^T \\ \ldots \\ k_5 Q_2^T \end{bmatrix} = \begin{bmatrix} -0.2259 & -0.0405 & 0.4850 \\ 0.0958 & 0.0172 & -0.2058 \\ -0.3046 & -0.0546 & 0.6541 \\ -0.3435 & -0.0615 & 0.7377 \\ 0.1015 & 0.0182 & -0.2180 \end{bmatrix}.$$

Fig. 3.2 shows the cross-sections of the controllable region (solid lines) in the planes of two state variables. The controllable region and the stability region for the maximum stabilizer $u(t) = \text{sat}(K_{max}x(t))$ coincide.

The linear-quadratic regulator (LQR) minimizing the following performance index

$$J = \int_0^\infty (x^T(t)x(t) + u^T(t)u(t))dt \tag{3.11}$$

has been synthesized for comparison purposes. The LQR stability region boundaries (dashed lines) have been computed by direct closed-loop system simulation and they are shown in Fig. 3.2 (see the top and the left middle plots). One can see that the stability region for the maximum stabilizer approximately three times bigger than for the LQR. In the bottom plots in Fig.3.2 several trajectories of the closed-loop system with LQR and maximum stabilizer controllers are shown to illustrate the size of stability regions.

3.4 Controller design for two-dimensional case

In this case the unstable subsystem is described by a second-order linear system

$$\dot{z}(t) = A_z z(t) + B_z u(t),$$

where $A_z \in R^2$, $B_z \in R^{2\times m}$, $u(t) \in U$ and $z(t) = Q^T{}_2\, x(t)$.

The design objectives in this case are similar to the previous design with one real eigenvalue. A saturated linear controller u = sat(Kz) has to stabilize the closed-loop system in the absence of control saturation and prevent leaving the controllable region when the system operates close to its boundary. We will consider a *null-controllable* set $C(T)$ with enough large T as an approximation of the controllable region C.

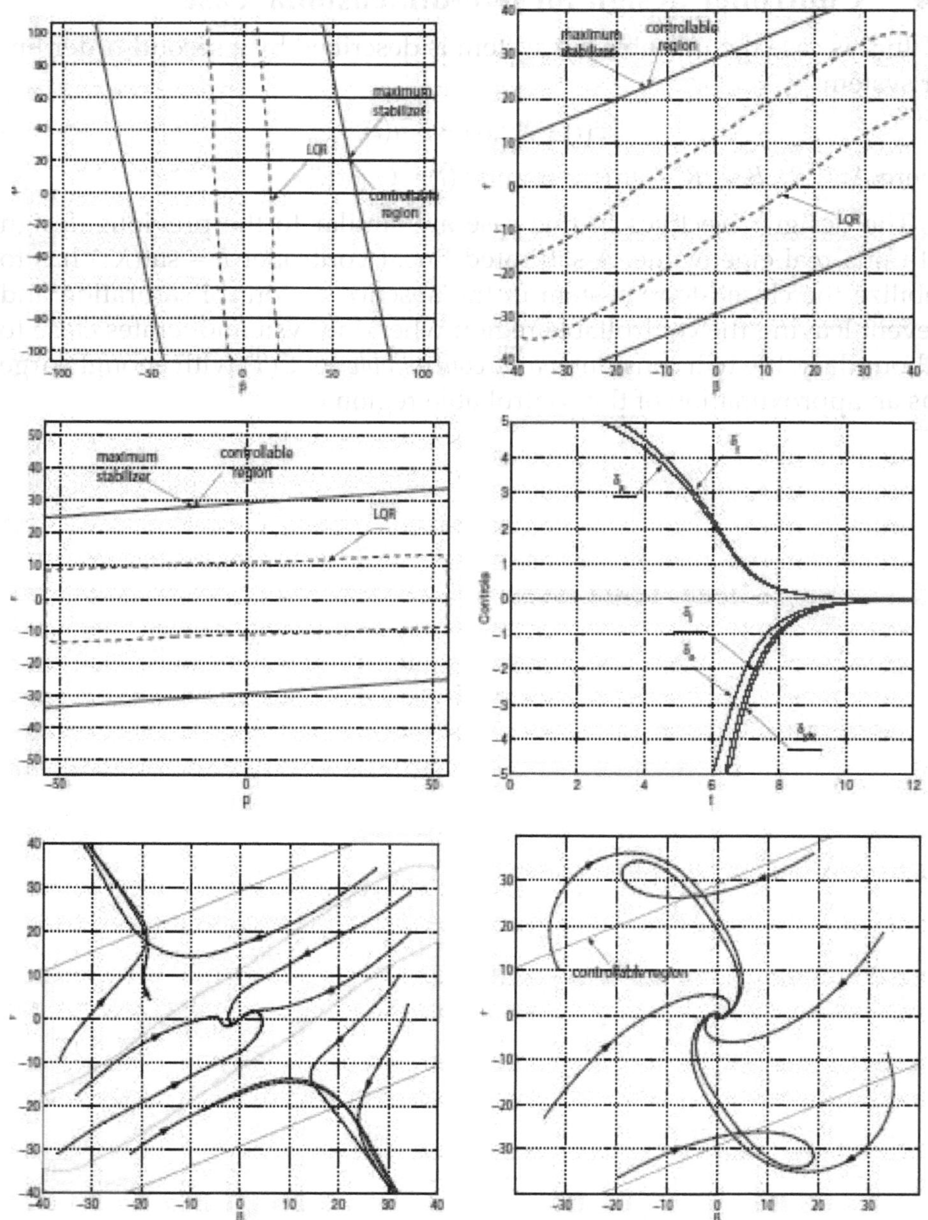

Figure 3.2: Cross-sections of stability regions for maximum stabilizer and linear-quadratic regulator (LQR), example of control functions produced by maximum stabilizer (middle right plot), closed-loop system trajectories for LQR (bottom left plot) and maximum stabilizer (bottom right plot) in (β,r) plane. All variables are given in degrees and degrees per second.

As a part of the control design method we utilize here Formalsky's method from the previous chapter (Formalsky, 1968).

At every boundary point of $C(T)$ the control function following (2.10) is expressed in the form of a relay law:

$$u^{(i)}(0) = u^{(i)}_{max}\text{sign}(-d^T b_{zi}), i = \overline{1, m}, \tag{3.12}$$

where d is a vector normal to the boundary of $C(T)$ at this point.

Each component of the control vector takes on the boundary of $C(T)$ its positive or negative extreme value and there are some points, where it changes sign. Because any *null-controllable* set is symmetrical, the points on the boundary of $C(T)$, where the control changes sign are also symmetrical.

These points $\pm z_{0_i}$ for every component $u^{(i)}$ of the control vector are defined by the condition that the vectors $\pm d_i$ (locally perpendicular to the boundary of $C(T)$ at these points) are also perpendicular the to controllability vector b_{zi}, i.e. $d_i^T b_{zi} = 0$ (see Fig. 3.3).

A relay control law

$$u^{(i)}(z) = u^{(i)}_{max}\text{sign}(k_i^T z), i = \overline{1, m}, \tag{3.13}$$

where k_i are vectors normal to the switch lines passing through $\pm z_{0i}$, can produce at every boundary point of $C(T)$ the same direction of the control vector as in (3.12) and therefore prevent the system moving outside of $C(T)$. The direction of k_i is defined from the inequality $k_i^T b_{zi} < 0$. In this case the control vector $b_{zi}u^{(i)}(z)$ will "push" the system state towards the interior of the controllable region.

Now consider the linear control law constructed from the relay control law (3.13):

$$u^{(i)} = \gamma|k_i|z, \qquad \text{where} \qquad |k_i| = \frac{u^{(i)}_{max}}{||k_i||_2}k_i^T. \tag{3.14}$$

In the presence of control deflection constraints, the control functions become nonlinear and can be expressed as:

$$u^{(i)}(z) = \text{sat}(\gamma|k_i|z), i = \overline{1, m}$$

The switching lines of the relay control law (3.13) in the phase plane, defined by $k^T_i z = 0$, are transformed into "strips", where the closed-loop system is free from control saturation and therefore linear.

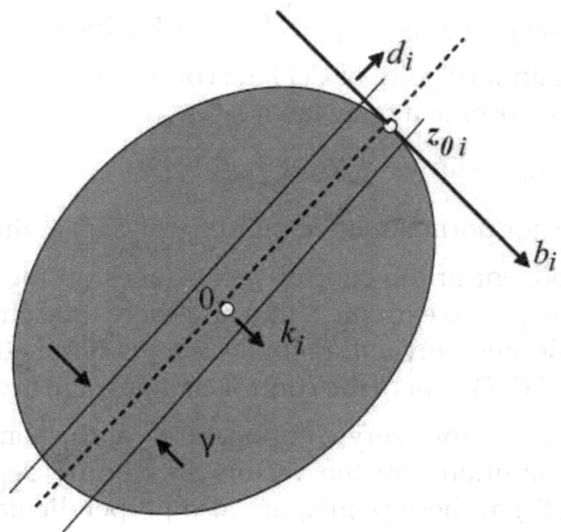

Figure 3.3: The main geometrical idea (ellipse represents the controllable region)

Parameter γ, which is the same for all control components, allows for variation of the width of these "strips" and thus for the compromise between the local stability characteristics expressed in terms of eigenvalues location and the size of the closed-loop system stability region. Of course, the stability region of this saturated linear control law is less than the controllable region and can asymptotically approach it only as $\gamma \to \infty$. That is why we call the controller "suboptimal".

Moreover, we can use the following well-known LMI inequalities (Boyd, Ghaoui, Feron and Balakrishnan, 1994) to express sufficient stability conditions:

$$A_z Q + QA^T_z - B_z B^T_z < 0 \tag{3.15}$$

$$\gamma K = -\tfrac{1}{2} B^T_z Q^{-1} \tag{3.16}$$

where

$$K = \begin{bmatrix} |k_1| \\ ... \\ |k_m| \end{bmatrix} \tag{3.17}$$

and Q-positive definite matrix parameter.

We can transform (3.16) as

$$KQ = -\frac{\beta}{2} B_z^T \tag{3.18}$$

where $\beta = 1/\gamma$. Clearly (3.15) and (3.18) are linear matrix inequalities and we can take $\beta \to 0$ instead of $\gamma \to \infty$ as our optimization goal.

These inequalities can be combined with other LMI-based performance conditions, thus providing us with a tool for control law design combining stability and performance characteristics.

It should be noted that the poles of the closed-loop system may approach the boundary between stable and unstable complex half-planes as $\gamma \to \infty$. This may result in a so called "fragile" control law, i.e. small changes in the A and B matrices can make the closed-loop system unstable. This usually means we need to somehow constrain γ from above.

To avoid this problem, one might calculate some kind of "stability radius" in parameter space when the synthesis is finished, reduce the upper limit for γ, if it is not enough, and recalculate the control law.

As a design example, consider the longitudinal dynamics of an aircraft trimmed at altitude H = 25000 ft and Mach number M = 0.9 (Hartmann, Barrett and Greene, 1979; MathWorks, 2001*b*). The linearized system of motion equations has the following stability and controllability matrices:

$$[A|B] = \left[\begin{array}{cccccc|cc} -0.0226 & -36.6170 & -18.8970 & -32.0900 & 3.2509 & -0.7626 & 0 & 0 \\ 0.0001 & -1.8997 & 0.9831 & -0.0007 & -0.1708 & -0.0050 & 0 & 0 \\ 0.0123 & 11.7200 & -2.6316 & 0.0009 & -31.6040 & 22.3960 & 0 & 0 \\ 0 & 0 & 1 & 0 & 0 & 0 & 0 & 0 \\ 0 & 0 & 0 & 0 & -30 & 0 & 30 & 0 \\ 0 & 0 & 0 & 0 & 0 & -30 & 0 & 30 \end{array}\right]$$

The first part of the state vector consists of the aircraft's basic rigid body variables: perturbation in the forward velocity δV, the angle of attack α, the pitch rate q, and the pitch attitude angle θ. Two first-order lags $x^{(5)}$ and $x^{(6)}$ are appended to the state vector to represent actuators dynamics. The control variables δ_e and δ_c are signals sent to elevon and canard actuators:

$$u = [\delta_e, \delta_c]T,\ |\delta_e| \le 0.035\ rad,\ |\delta_c| \le 0.035\ rad.$$

Note that the angles and angular rates are expressed in radians and radians per second, respectively.

The system due to aircraft aerodynamic static instability has an oscillatory unstable mode in the phugoid frequency range, which can be separated off via the Schur decomposition:

$$[A_z|B_z] = \left[\begin{array}{cc|cc} 0.7067 & 2.6227 & 5.1766 & -3.6583 \\ -0.0237 & 0.6729 & 6.7815 & -4.6968 \end{array}\right],$$

$$z(t) = Q_2^T x(t), Q_2^T = \left[\begin{array}{cccccc} 0.0098 & -0.0377 & -0.1852 & -0.9589 & 0.1726 & -0.1219 \\ -0.0036 & -0.9269 & -0.2146 & 0.1385 & 0.2260 & -0.1566 \end{array}\right].$$

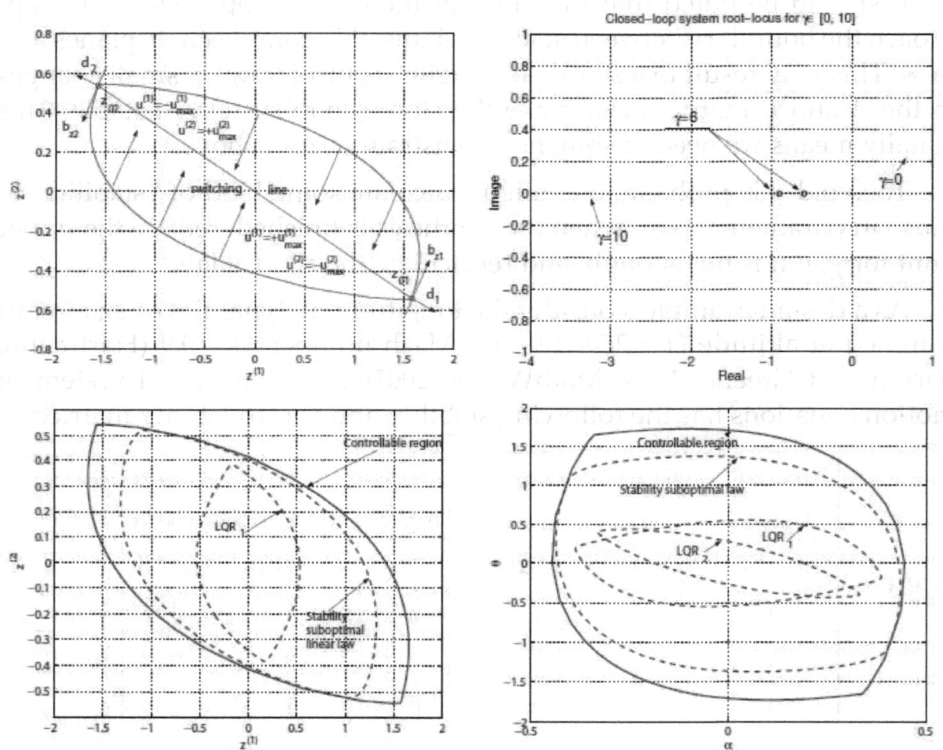

Figure 3.4: The relay law computation (top left plot), closed-loop system root locus (top right plot), stability and controllable regions for anti-stable subsystem (bottom left plot), cross-sections of stability regions in the plane (α, θ) (bottom right plot).

Using the Formalsky method, the *null-controllable* sets $C(T)$ have been computed until convergence to the boundary of controllable region C. In this example, the convergence process has been stopped at $T = 10$ sec. The controllable region boundary was approximated by 120 points.

To design a linear control law (3.14), the vectors *di* normal to the boundary of $C(10)$ at the points where the control functions change sign ($d^T_i\, b_{zi} =$

0, $i = 1, 2$), have been defined:

$$d_1 = [b_{z1}^{(2)}, -b_{z1}^{(1)}]^T = [6.7815, -5.1766]^T,$$
$$d_2 = [b_{z2}^{(2)}, -b_{z2}^{(1)}]^T = [-4.6968, 3.6583]^T.$$

Now the control switching points on the boundary of the controllable region, approximated by C(10), can be computed:

$$z_{01} = \arg\max_{z\in C(10)} d_1^T z = -0.035\sum_{i=1}^{2}\int_0^{10} e^{-A_z\tau} b_{zi}\mathrm{sign}(-d_1^T e^{-A_z\tau} b_{zi})d\tau = (1.5703, -0.5421)^T,$$

$$z_{02} = \arg\max_{z\in C(10)} d_2^T z = -0.035\sum_{i=1}^{2}\int_0^{10} e^{-A_z\tau} b_{zi}\mathrm{sign}(-d_2^T e^{-A_z\tau} b_{zi})d\tau = (-1.5703, 0.5421)^T.$$

In our case there are two switching lines passing through points $\pm z_{01}$ and $\pm z_{02}$ on the controllable region boundary, and these lines are numerically the same for each of the two controls (see Fig. 3.4, top left plot). These switching lines are described by equations:

$$k_1^T z = 0, \quad k_2^T z = 0$$

where k_i are defined as:

$$k_1 = [z_{01}^{(2)}, -z_{01}^{(1)}]^T = [-0.5421, -1.5703]^T,$$
$$k_2 = [z_{02}^{(2)}, -z_{02}^{(1)}]^T = [0.5421, 1.5703]^T.$$

Since $k^T_1 b_{z1} < 0$, $k^T_2 b_{z2} < 0$, these k_i already have correct signs.

In the top right plot in Fig. 3.4 the root-locus for the closed-loop system with control law (3.14) is shown for $\gamma = 0 \div 10$. Parameter $\gamma = 6$ is taken for the computation of the "stability suboptimal" control law.

In the state-space of original system this suboptimal control law has the form $u(x) = \mathrm{sat}(K_{sub}x)$, where

$$K_{sub} = \begin{bmatrix} 6\frac{0.035}{\|k_1\|_2} k_1^T Q_2^T \\ \\ 6\frac{0.035}{\|k_2\|_2} k_2^T Q_2^T \end{bmatrix} = \begin{bmatrix} 0 & 0.186 & 0.0552 & 0.0382 & -0.0566 & 0.0394 \\ 0 & -0.186 & -0.0552 & -0.0382 & 0.0566 & -0.0394 \end{bmatrix}$$

The comparison of the stability region for the designed "stability suboptimal" control law and the open-loop system controllable region is presented in the bottom left and right plots in Fig. 3.4 in the anti-stable subspace and in the physical plane (α, θ). It is clearly seen that the closed-loop system stability region with the designed linear control is rather close to the controllable region.

In the two bottom plots in Fig. 3.4 one can see also the cross-sections of the stability regions for the two linear quadratic regulators designed for comparison purposes. Linear quadratic regulators have been computed by minimizing the performance index (3.11): one considering only the unstable subspace (LQR_1) and another for the whole original system, thus including both stable and unstable subspaces (LQR_2).

One can see that the stability region for LQR_1 is bigger than the region for LQR_2, because LQR_1 stabilizes only the anti-stable subsystem, while LQR_2 allocates some control resourses for the stable subspace and leaves less for the unstable one. Meanwhile the designed stability suboptimal control law provides much a bigger stability region than both the linear quadratic regulators and its size is very close to the controllable region.

3.5 Conclusion

Stabilization of linearized dynamics with one anti-stable eigenvalue and a redundant number of control effectors can be performed in the whole controllable region by a saturated linear control law. The maximum stabilizer controller in the form of saturated linear feedback can be designed using the linear programming.

In the case of two unstable eigenvalues the maximum stabilizer can be designed only in the relay-type form. Nevertheless, the suboptimal linear saturated control law can always be found.

In the general case of higher-dimensional instability, the design of saturated linear law is impossible (Goebel, 2005) and the maximum stabilizer should be nonlinear even in the unsaturated region.

Chapter 4

Reconfigurable Control Allocation

In this chapter we study the control allocation problem, which arises in overdetermined control systems, i.e. systems with the number of controls greater than the number of system states. In the first part of the chapter we consider the set of all possible control actions that can be generated by the different allocation of available actuators in the linear case. We conclude that this set is actually a kind of polytope - a *zonotope*, and we describe its properties that we can use further for control purposes.

In the second part, we propose a novel real-time linear control allocation algorithm based on the ideas from *interval analysis* and zonotope properties. The algorithm yields the solution in a finite number of iterations with any given accuracy. It can be therefore considered for implementation in safety critical applications that may require reconfiguration possibility due to control effector damage.

4.1 Introduction

The general idea of the reconfigurable control allocation is that all fault detection and reconfiguration capabilities are concentrated in one special unit called the *control allocator*, while the general control algorithm, which is producing a virtual control input, remains intact. In the case of an actuator fault, only the control allocation unit needs to be reconfigured and in many cases it can generate the same virtual control vector using a different set of control effectors (see Fig. 4.1). The control allocation (not necessarily reconfigurable) has been attracting much attention in the aerospace community for around 15 years since the first algorithm of this type - the so called direct allocation approach (Durham, 1993; Durham, 1994). Recently, the problem appeared in the context of general control theory. In the aeronautical context, the role of virtual controls is usually played by moments and forces.

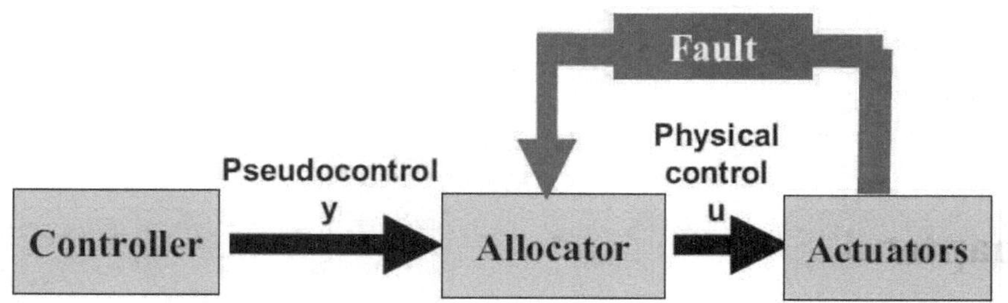

Figure 4.1: Reconfigurable control allocation approach

In the sequel we will use the assumption that a linear relationship exists between the n-dimensional pseudo-control vector $y \in R^n$ and the actual control effector displacements $u \in R^m$, $n < m$, i.e.

$$y = Bu, \tag{4.1}$$

where $B = [b_1 | b_2 | ... | b_m]$ is the control effectiveness matrix having m columns. This formu-lation may arise either from the assumption of linearity of moments and forces produced by aerodynamic control surfaces, or otherwise from the use of local slopes at the current operating point (Doman and Oppenheimer, 2002). The pseudo-control vector in the aeronautical applications may include commanded moment/forces and any additional state variables, introduced for stabilization purposes.

The problem of determining u for a given y is the root-finding problem, and all allocation algorithms actually differ one from another by the root-finding method. The simplest solution would be to apply a pseudo-inverse matrix, but this does not necessarily guarantee optimality of the solution - not all possible control actions in this case could be realized, because the control effectors are supposed to be limited by some minimal and maximal values:

$$u \in U,\ U = \{u \in R^m : u^{(i)}{}_{min} \le u^{(i)} \le u^{(i)}{}_{max},\ i = \overline{1, m}\} \tag{4.2}$$

The achievable pseudo-control vectors are then confined to some *attainable pseudo-control set* (APS) Y :

$$Y(U) = \{y : y = Bu,\ u \in U\} \tag{4.3}$$

The on-board implementation of a control allocation algorithm needs to be computationally effective and should always converge to a solution. Therefore, many optimal methods that might be easily applicable and reconfigurable off-line, like linear or quadratic programming (Bodson, 2002), may not constitute a reasonable engineering solution to the problem (Cameron and Princen, 2000). The latest modifications of the direct allocation approach (Petersen and Bodson, 2002) and methods based on approximations or explicit representations of mathematical programming solutions (Johansen, Fossen and Tondel, 2005; Gaulocher, Roos and Cumer, 2007) are indeed computationally effective, but lack in reconfiguration capability — in the case of failure the re-computation of the whole allocator unit is needed.

In this chapter we introduce a new root-finding method that was first outlined for 2D and 3D control allocation tasks in (Demenkov, 2005) — a method of *generalized interval bisection*. We propose a novel n-dimensional real-time linear control allocation algorithm that satisfies three criteria:

1. guarantee of convergence to a solution
2. a known upper bound for time to find a solution
3. numerical properties such that the size of errors can be controlled

For any given accuracy, a control effectiveness matrix B and a pseudo-control vector y, the algorithm yields the solution u in a finite number of iterations, while utilizing the whole attainable pseudo-control set $Y(U)$. The complexity of the algorithm is less than for optimization-based methods or direct allocation. Moreover, during the iterations the volume of the search space decreases exponentially and the number of required basic operations is proportional to the logarithm of the reciprocal of the accuracy. The control allocator based on this algorithm is therefore easily adaptable to any changes in control effectiveness and even effector damage.

The drawback of the proposed algorithm is that it does not optimize the solution using any additional performance criteria. Therefore it might be considered as a "last resort" in a system usually governed by some other (optimal) control allocation algorithm, to keep the system functioning in situations where safety comes first after an actuator failure.

4.2 Interval bisection

4.2.1 One-dimensional bisection

Let us recall the simple idea of the bisection method for a function of one variable. Over some interval the function is known to pass through zero because it changes sign. Evaluate the function at the interval's midpoint and examine its sign. Use the midpoint to replace whichever limit has the same sign. After each iteration the bounds containing the root decrease by a factor of two. If after i iterations the root is known to be within an interval of size $\varepsilon_i = b_i - a_i$ (see Fig. 4.2), then after the next iteration it will be bracketed within an interval of size

$$\varepsilon_{i+1} = \varepsilon_i/2. \tag{4.4}$$

Thus, we know in advance the number of iterations N required to achieve a given tolerance in the solution:

$$\Delta \approx \frac{\varepsilon_0}{2^N} \Rightarrow N \approx \log_2 \frac{\varepsilon_0}{\Delta}, \tag{4.5}$$

where ε_0 is the size of the initial interval, Δ is the desired ending tolerance.

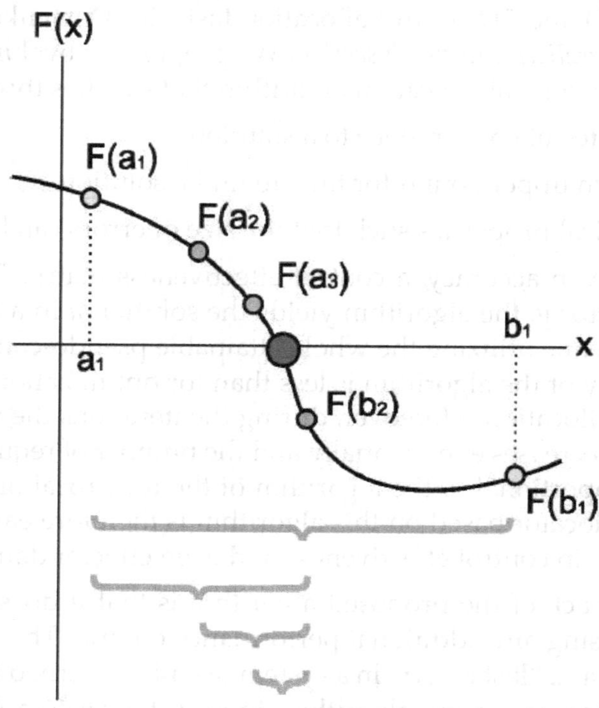

Figure 4.2: Bisection method for one variable function (courtesy of Wikipedia)

4.2.2 Generalized (n-dimensional) interval bisection

This classical bisection method can be generalized for n-dimensional problems, and has been extensively studied in the context of the so called *interval analysis* (Jaulin, Kieffer, Didrit and Walter, 2001). Nevertheless, in general it is impossible to construct its generalization in the same way as for the one-dimensional case, because it is hard to prove that the generalized interval in n dimensions does not contain any solution. The number of intervals potentially containing a solution is then growing exponentially and this restricts the applicability of the approach.

In our case, however, it is possible, and the one-dimensional version of the algorithm can be generalized in the following way. Notice that (4.2) defines a box U in the Euclidean space R^m of all possible control vectors u. In other words, it defines a subset of the control space that is overall bounded by hyperplanes orthogonal to the axes of coordinates. Suppose that we have a method to determine if the given pseudo-control vector y is inside the attainable pseudo-control set for the given box. Then we cut the box U into two boxes U_1 and U_2 by half-splitting it along the coordinate direction, in which U is longest. We check each box for the ability to generate the given pseudo-control vector, replace U by one of the two new boxes that has y in its APS, and repeat the procedure, constructing the diminishing sequence of boxes:

$$U \leftarrow \begin{cases} U_1, \text{ if } y \in Y(U_1); \\ U_2, \text{ if } y \in Y(U_2). \end{cases} \tag{4.6}$$

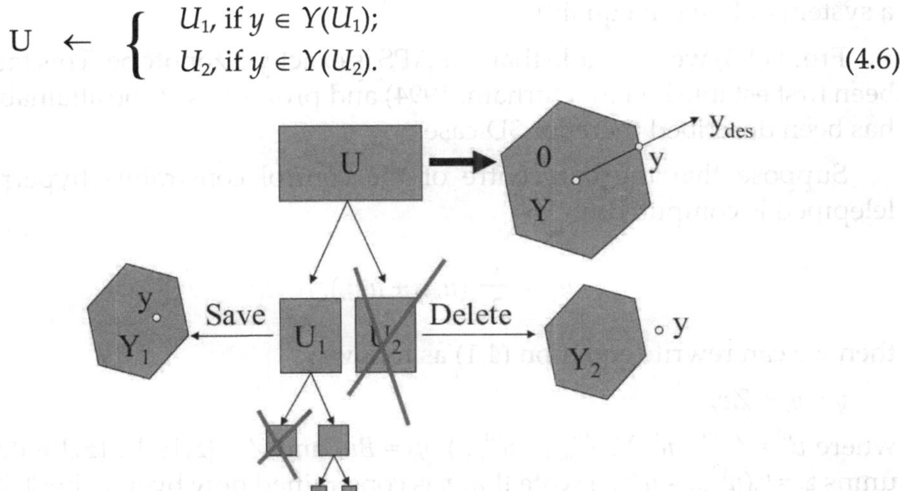

Figure 4.3: The idea of our bisection algorithm

After m steps of this procedure, we will have the longest facet of U two times less than for the original box. So, if we specify in the same way some tolerance Δ for the longest facet of the box, we will obtain the solution in Nm bisection steps, where N is given by (4.5) if we treat ε_0 as the length of the longest facet of the initial box:

$$\varepsilon_0 = \max_{i=\overline{1,m}} \{u_{max}^{(i)} - u_{min}^{(i)}\}. \tag{4.7}$$

To guarantee the convergence to a solution, we must guarantee that a given pseudo-control vector y_{des} belongs to the APS of the initial box. For this, one can check the vector and replace it by some vector y lying on the APS boundary, if it violates the constraints. The easiest way to do so is to just scale the given y_{des} preserving its direction, like in the direct allocation approach (see Fig. 4.3).

It is possible that both U_1 and U_2 contain the solution. In this case, one can apply some optimality criteria to decide which box will be deleted. For example, we can choose a box that has inside the previously generated control vector u, to minimize the distance between two consequently generated control vectors.

4.3 Properties of the attainable pseudo-control set

In (Ziegler, 1995) we can find the definition of a *zonotope*: it is the image of a cube under an affine projection. Zonotopes are special polytopes. We recall that a polytope can be described both by the set of its vertices and by a system of linear inequalities.

From (4.3) we conclude that our APS is exactly a zonotope. This fact has been first established in (Durham, 1994) and properties of the attainable set has been described there for 3D case.

Suppose that the barycentre of the control constraints hyperparallelepiped is computed:

$$u_0 = \frac{1}{2}(u_{min} + u_{max}),$$

then we can rewrite equation (4.1) as follows:

$$y = y_0 + Zv, \tag{4.8}$$

where $v^{(i)} = (u^{(i)} - u^{(i)}{}_0)/(u^{(i)}{}_{max} - u^{(i)}{}_{min})$, $y_0 = Bu_0$ and $Z = [z_1 | z_2 | \dots | z_m]$ with columns $z_i = b_i(u^{(i)}{}_{max} - u^{(i)}{}_{min})$ Note that v is constrained now by m-cube: $\|v\|_\infty \le 1$.

Definition 5 *A zonotope is the image of a cube under an affine projection, that is, a polytope $Y \subseteq R^n$ of the form*

$$Y = \{y \in R^n : y = y_0 + \sum_{i=1}^{m} z_i v^{(i)}, -1 \le v^{(i)} \le 1\}$$

for some matrix $Z = [z_1 | z_2 | \dots | z_m] \in R^{n\times m}$.

Without loss of generality, in the sequel we suppose $y0 = 0$ in the last definition.

The following two basic theorems are our reformulation of theorems from (McMullen and Shepard, 1971).

Theorem 3 *Let y_i, $i = \overline{1, N}$ be vertices of a polytope Y in the Euclidean space. Then any point $y \in Y$ can be written in the form*

$$y = \sum_{i=1}^{N} \lambda_i y_i, \quad \lambda_i \geq 0, \quad \sum_{i=1}^{N} \lambda_i = 1,$$

that is, a convex combination of y_i.

This theorem has its dual one:

Theorem 4 *Let* $\{y_i\}_{i=\overline{1,N}}$ *be any set of points in the Euclidean space and*

$$y = \sum_{i=1}^{N} \lambda_i y_i, \quad \lambda_i \geq 0, \quad \sum_{i=1}^{N} \lambda_i = 1,$$

that is, a convex combination of yi. Then $y \in Y$ *where Y is a polytope with vertices from the set of points yi.*

This means that some but not all vertices of the polytope Y are from this set, while other y_i are inside Y and therefore redundant for its representation.

Consider now v as a convex combination of some vertices v_i, $i = \overline{1, M}$. Such represen-tation always exists because v is limited to the hypercube H in R^m:

$$H = \{v \in R^m : \|v\|_\infty \leq 1\}. \tag{4.9}$$

The vertices of this hypercube contain only extremal values in its components, i.e.

$v_i^{(j)} = \pm 1,\ j = \overline{1, m},\ i = \overline{1, M}.$

Theorem 5 *The components of v corresponding to a vertex of Y have only extremal values.*

Proof: From the Theorem 3, Y is defined as

$$y = \sum_{i=1}^{M} \lambda_i Z v_i,$$

i.e. it is a convex combination of Zv_i points and from Theorem 4 any vertex of Y is represented by Zv_i, where v_i is a vertex of the hypercube H.

Now we are ready to introduce the main results of this section. These results are in the form of simple formulas, which allow us to determine all facets and vertices of the polytope Y that is defined in the two- and three-dimensional Euclidean space.

4.3.1 3D case

The following result first appeared in (Petersen and Bodson, 2000) without proof. Now we give the complete proof of the result and discuss some related computational problems.

Theorem 6 *Suppose* $n = 3$. *Then any normal vector of a facet of the polytope* Y *is a scaled cross product of some two columns taken from the matrix* Z.

Proof: Consider the following optimization task:

$$d^T y \to \max,$$
$$y \in Y,$$

where d is a normal vector of the polytope facet. From linear programming theory, it is well known that the problem solution set will always include all vertices that are incident to this facet (Dantzig, 1966). Consider only these vertices as the solutions to the problem. We can rewrite the goal function as a function of the variable v :

$$f(v) = d^T y(v) = \sum_{j=1}^{m} d^T z_j v^{(j)},$$

and then our optimization task is

$$f(v) \to \max,$$
$$v \in H.$$

Note that

$$f(v) \leq \sum_{j=1}^{m} \sup_{v}(d^T z_j v^{(j)}) = \sum_{j=1}^{m} d^T z_j v_{ext}^{(j)} = f(v_{ext}),$$

where $v_{ext}^{(j)}$ has the form:

$$v_{ext}^{(j)} = \operatorname{sign}(d^T z_j), \text{ if } d^T z_j \neq 0;$$
$$v_{ext}^{(j)} \in [-1, 1], \text{ if } d^T z_j = 0.$$

It is clear that since

$$f(v) \leq f(v_{ext})$$

and varying any $v_{ext}^{(j)}$ in the case of $d^T z_j = 0$ does not change the value of $f(v_{ext})$, these v_{ext} are the solutions to our optimization task.

From Theorem 5, it is clear that since we consider only those v_{ext} that correspond to the vertices of Y, these v_{ext} have the form:

$$v_{ext}^{(j)} = \begin{cases} \text{sign}(d^T z_j), & d^T z_j \neq 0; \\ \pm 1, & d^T z_j = 0. \end{cases} \tag{4.10}$$

The number N_0 of zero entries in the $d^T Z$ row vector defines the number of vertices N_v, which are the solution to our optimization task:

$$N_v = 2^{N_0}.$$

Recall that a facet of a polytope in 3D space contains at least three vertices. It is clear that in the case of no zeros in the row vector $d^T Z$, only one vertex serves as a solution and therefore d is not a facet normal vector. One zero in $d^T Z$ corresponds to only two vertices and d still cannot be a normal vector of a facet. In the case of two zeros in $d^T Z$ we will have d, which is uniquely defined as the vector orthogonal to at least two columns of Z. And it is now a normal vector of a facet, because it corresponds to at least four vertices of Y.

It is worth looking now at Fig. 4.4 in order to understand the principles of the proof.

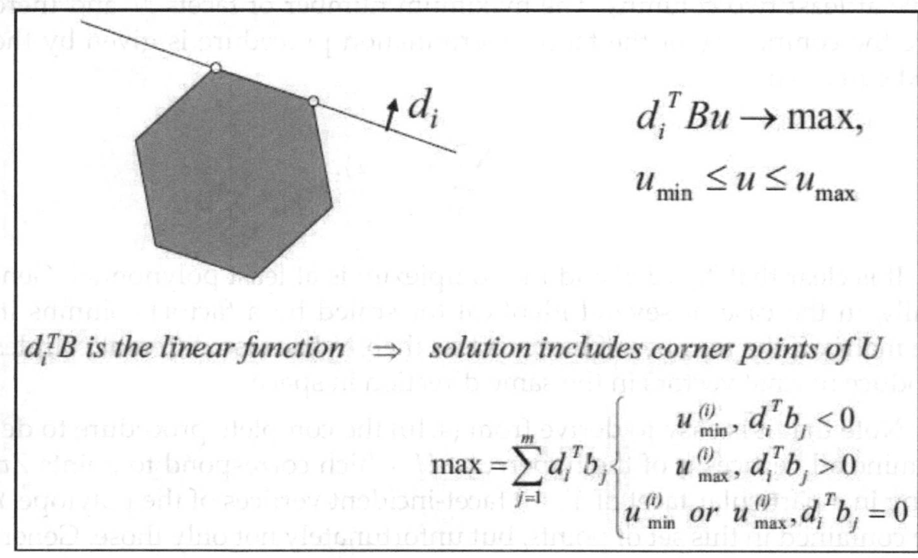

Figure 4.4: Schema of the Theorem 6 proof using the original variables

Any normal vector d of a polytope facet is computed as the cross product of two different columns z_i and z_j taken from the matrix Z:

$$d^{(1)} = z_i^{(2)} z_j^{(3)} - z_i^{(3)} z_j^{(2)},$$

$$d^{(2)} = z_i^{(3)} z_j^{(1)} - z_i^{(1)} z_j^{(3)},$$

$$d^{(3)} = z_i^{(1)} z_j^{(2)} - z_i^{(2)} z_j^{(1)}.$$

Note that for any facet normal vector d there exists its opposite in sign vector $-d$, which is defined as the normal vector of the opposite facet. Because of this, our polytope is a symmetric one.

Suppose that we have all columns of Z in a list and determine all pairs of one column z_i and any other column of Z from the list; the number of such pairs is $m - 1$ and any pair gives us two valid facets of the polytope. In the next step, we have to remove this z_i from the list and repeat the procedure (now the number of pairs is $m - 2$). Proceed the same way until we have at least two columns. The maximum number of facets N_f and there fore the complexity of the facet determination procedure is given by the next equation:

$$N_f = 2\sum_{i=1}^{m}(m - i).$$

It is clear that $N_f < 2m^2$ and the complexity is at least polynomial. Generally, in the case of several identical (or scaled by a factor) columns in the matrix Z the number of facets is less than N_f because different couples produce normal vectors in the same direction in space.

Note that it is easy to derive from (4.10) the complete procedure to determine all vertices v_i of the hypercube H, which correspond to points Zv_i lying in a particular facet of Y. All facet-incident vertices of the polytope Y are contained in this set of points, but unfortunately not only those. Generally, some points Zv_i exist, which are *not* related to the vertices of Y but are placed on the same facet. In this case, we need a procedure to determine only those vertices of H that correspond to the vertices of Y.

This procedure is as follows, based on the fact that we have at least three incident facets for any "true" vertex of Y.

- For each facet of Y, create a list of those H-vertices v_i that correspond to those points Zv_i that belong to this facet.
- Create one global list of such vertices and associate with any vertex a counter, taking a vertex from local lists only if it is not already in the global list. If it is in the list, just increase the counter associated with this vertex (set counter to one initially).
- Remove from the global list any vertex having a counter value less than 3.

The rest of the global list contains only those vertices of H that correspond to the "true" vertices of Y.

For each particular facet, incident vertices must be ordered clockwise or counterclockwise to draw this facet of the polytope Y.

We can split a polytope into tetrahedra having exactly four vertices with one of them at the origin (we suppose that the origin lies not on the polytope boundary, this is always the case while we consider the polytope Y here). Then, the volume of a tetrahedron with

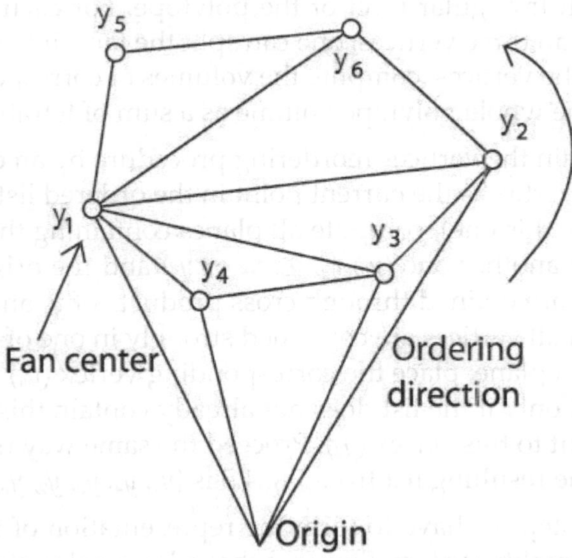

Figure 4.5: Reordering procedure.

nonzero vertices y_i, y_j, y_k is given by (Rourke, 1994)

$$\frac{1}{6}\det\left(\begin{bmatrix} y_i^{(1)} & y_i^{(2)} & y_i^{(3)} & 1 \\ y_j^{(1)} & y_j^{(2)} & y_j^{(3)} & 1 \\ y_k^{(1)} & y_k^{(2)} & y_k^{(3)} & 1 \\ 0 & 0 & 0 & 1 \end{bmatrix}\right).$$

This volume is signed and is positive if $\{y_i, y_j, y_k\}$ form a counterclockwise circuit when viewed from the side away from the origin, so that the facet normal, determined by the right-hand rule, points towards the outside.

Given a clockwise or counterclockwise ordered list of vertices for a polytope facet, one can triangulate this facet as a "fan" with all diagonals incident to a common vertex and this may be done with any vertex serving as the fan "centre" (the point y_1 in Fig. 4.5). The volume of a polytope may be computed by summing the volumes of tetrahedra constructed from the origin and each triangular facet of the polytope. For each polytope facet having more than three vertices, one can split the facet into triangular ones by reordering the vertices, compute the volumes of corresponding tetrahedra and then the whole polytope volume as a sum of tetrahedra volumes.

Let us explain the vertices reordering procedure by an example in Fig. 4.5. Given any vertex as the current point in the ordered list (which initially contains only this one), compute all planes containing three points: this vertex (y_1), any another one (y_2, y_3, y_4, y_5 or y_6) and the origin. Clearly, all of these planes are defined through cross products of y_1 and one of $\{y_2, y_3, y_4, y_5, y_6\}$. When all vertices are contained strongly in one of the half-spaces determined by a plane, place the corresponding vertex (y_4) as the next one in the list (do it only if the list does not already contain this one). Then set the current point to this vertex (y_4). Proceed the same way until all vertices are ordered. The resulting list from Fig.4.5 is $\{y_1, y_4, y_3, y_2, y_6, y_5\}$.

At the last step we have to form the representation of the polytope Y via a linear inequality system. Suppose that all normal vectors d_j, $j = \overline{1, N}$ of the polytope facets are collected in matrix D with rows d^T_j. For each d_j we can determine the distance of the corresponding facet from the origin. Let us take for each facet any incident vertex y_i. Then, this distance is given by the next equation:

$$h^{(j)} = d_j^T y_i.$$

The vector h of such distances allows us to write a representation of the polytope Y in a linear inequality form:

$$Y = \{y \in R^n : Dy \le h\}. \tag{4.11}$$

It is easy to see that in the case of $y_0 \ne 0$ the modified polytope Y has the following representation:

$$\Omega = \{y \in R^n : Dy \le h + Dy_0\}.$$

Also, all vertices of the modified polytope Y are constructed from vertices y_i of the previous polytope as $y_0 + y_i$. The volume of Y is independent of this coordinate shift.

4.3.2 2D case

The planar case is much simpler in its computational aspect. The following theorem is the counterpart of Theorem 6 for two-dimensional space.

Theorem 7 *Suppose $n = 2$. Then any normal vector of the polytope facet is orthogonal to some column taken from the matrix Z.*

Proof: Proceed the same way as in Theorem 6. Note that in the planar case any polytope facet has no more than two vertices (and no less, of course). In the case of one zero in d^TZ we will have d, which is uniquely defined as the vector orthogonal to at least one column of Z. Also it is a normal vector of a facet, because it corresponds to at least two vertices of Y.

The computation of the vector d, which is orthogonal to a particular vector z_i taken from the matrix Z, is rather simple and given by the following formulas:

$$d^{(1)} = -z_i^{(2)},\ d^{(2)} = z_i^{(1)}.$$

Half of the maximum number of facets in this case is equal to a number of rows in the matrix Z, i.e. $N_f = 2m$.

The procedure for determining "true" vertices of the polytope is generally the same, but in this case we have to remove vertices with counter value less than 2.

There is no need to reorder the vertices in the planar case, each facet has exactly two incident vertices and the volume (which is actually an area in the planar case) of a triangle formed by these vertices and the origin is as follows (Rourke, 1994):

$$\frac{1}{2}(a^{(1)}b^{(2)} - a^{(2)}b^{(1)}),$$

here we denote vertices as a and b (labeled counterclockwise).

The area of a two-dimensional polytope (which is obviously named as the *polygon*) is computed as the sum of all such triangles. Also, to represent a polytope in linear inequality form (4.11) we have to proceed the same way as in the previous subsection.

4.4 Control allocation algorithm

Now, we return to our main goal - using the described properties of the APS and the ideology of interval bisection, solve the control allocation task in real-time.

The sketch of an algorithm that implements the generalized bisection method is as follows. First, we construct from the given matrix B some kind of *indicator function,* which will quickly give us an answer regarding as to whether or not the given pseudo-control vector is inside the attainable pseudo-control set for the particular box. For this, we use the representation of the APS in the form of a system of linear inequalities. Second, we scale the given pseudo-control vector to guarantee it is inside the APS for the initial box. Third, we apply bisection iterations to obtain the solution. All these steps are performed in a predetermined and finite number of floating-point operations.

4.4.1 Construction of the indicator function

Let us suppose that in the general case every normal vector d_k to a facet of the APS is orthogonal to some $n-1$ columns $b_{k_1}, b_{k_2}, \ldots, b_{k_{n-1}}$ taken from the matrix B if $\text{rank}([b_{k_1} \mid b_{k_2} \mid \ldots \mid b_{k_{n-1}}]) = n-1$.

Note also that for every such vector an opposite-direction vector exists that is perpendicular to another APS facet (since the APS is symmetrical). So, we can easily compute d_k for all possible non-degenerate combinations of $n-1$ columns of matrix B and be sure that we have caught all directions perpendicular to APS facets. The particular magnitude of these vectors is not important for our procedure (i.e. we do not need to normalize them first).

It is clear that the number of APS facets is bounded above by the number M of vectors d_k, which is the number of combinations of $n-1$ vectors out of a set of m:

$$M = \binom{m}{n-1} = \frac{(m)!}{(m-n+1)!(n-1)!}.$$

Some of generated vectors are normals to a facet, and some may be redundant. But the amazing property of the linear inequality approach is that we can use all of them to produce a correct APS representation.

Assume that we want to maximize a linear function ${d^T}_k y$ over the whole APS for the given box of control constraints U defined by (4.2):

$$\text{dist}(U, d_k) = \max_{y \in Y(U)} d_k^T y. \tag{4.12}$$

The maximization over vectors y can be easily replaced by the maximization over control variables:

$$\text{dist}(U, d_k) = \max_{u \in U} d_k^T Bu = \max_{u \in U} \sum_{i=1}^{m} d_k^T b_i u^{(i)}, \tag{4.13}$$

and we can maximize this sum by maximizing each of the summands separately:

$$\text{dist}(U, d_k) = \sum_{i=1}^{m} \max\{d_k^T b_i u_{min}^{(i)}, d_k^T b_i u_{max}^{(i)}\}. \tag{4.14}$$

Let us formally construct the *indicator function* $I_U(y)$, which is *TRUE* if vector y belongs to the APS for the given box U or *FALSE* otherwise. Then $I_U(y) \equiv$ *TRUE* if and only if y satisfies the following system of linear inequalities:

$$\left.\begin{array}{l} d_k^T y \leq \text{dist}(U, d_k), \quad k = \overline{1, M} \\ -d_k^T y \leq \text{dist}(U, -d_k), k = \overline{1, M} \end{array}\right\} \tag{4.15}$$

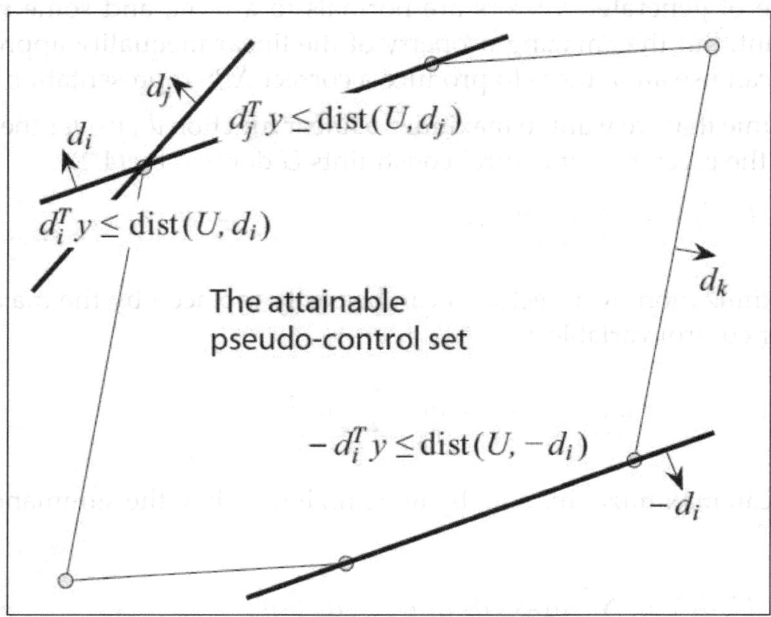

Figure 4.6: APS represented by a set of linear inequalities.

It can be seen in Fig. 4.6 how this system defines the APS. Here d_i is a true normal vector to a facet, while d_j is redundant for the representation (but its presence does not affect it).

4.4.2 Scaling the pseudo-control vector

If the APS for the initial box contains the origin, one can construct the following scalar nonnegative *Minkowski function* (Blanchini, 1995) induced by the APS:

$$V(y) = \max_k \max\{d_k^T y/\text{dist}(U, d_k), -d_k^T y/\text{dist}(U, -d_k)\}. \tag{4.16}$$

Its level surfaces are obtained by scaling the boundary of the APS (and it is equal to 1 at the boundary). For those y that violate the APS it allows the scaled pseudo-control vector αy lying on the boundary and pointing in the same direction to be easily computed. For this, one can take

$$\alpha = 1/V(y). \tag{4.17}$$

4.4.3 Splitting the control box

This is the easiest step of the algorithm. Suppose that we have some control box U defined as in (4.2). Then we can find the coordinate direction in which U has the longest facet:

$$k = \arg \max_{i=\overline{1,m}} \{u_{max}^{(i)} - u_{min}^{(i)}\} \tag{4.18}$$

Now we can form two adjacent boxes splitting the interval for k-th coordinate in the middle:

$$u_0^{(k)} = (u_{max}^{(k)} + u_{min}^{(k)})/2$$

$$U_1 = \{u \in R^m :\ u_{min}^{(1)} \le u^{(1)} \le u_{max}^{(1)}, ...,$$
$$u_{min}^{(k)} \le u^{(k)} \le u_0^{(k)}, ..., u_{min}^{(m)} \le u^{(m)} \le u_{max}^{(m)}\}$$
$$U_2 = \{u \in R^m :\ u_{min}^{(1)} \le u^{(1)} \le u_{max}^{(1)}, ...,$$
$$u_0^{(k)} \le u^{(k)} \le u_{max}^{(k)}, ..., u_{min}^{(m)} \le u^{(m)} \le u_{max}^{(m)}\} \tag{4.19}$$

During the iterations, one of these boxes should be deleted and the other one will replace U.

4.4.4 The algorithm

Now we are ready to implement all the steps of the algorithm in one piece of a pseudocode, which will receive as input parameters the required pseudo-control vector y_{des}, the previous control value u_0, the normals to facets d_k, $k = \overline{1, M}$, the initial control box U and the number N of required iterations (precomputed with the help of (4.5)):

if $V(y_{des}) > 1$ **then** $y = y_{des}/V(y_{des})$ else $y = y_{des}$

for $i = 1$ **to** Nm

  Split U **into** U_1 **and** U_2

  Compute $I_{U_1}(y)$ **and** $I_{U_2}(y)$

  if $I_{U_1}(y) \equiv TRUE$ **and** $I_{U_2}(y_0) \equiv TRUE$

    if $u_0 \in U_1$ **then** $U = U_1$ **else** $U = U_1$

  else

    if $I_{U_1}(y) \equiv TRUE$ then $U = U_1$ else $U = U_2$

  end

end

In the case of ambiguity this algorithm tries to pick the solution closer to the previous control vector u_0. Every u in the resulting box U is acceptable since it has the required numerical accuracy. One can take the center of the box as a final solution.

Note that in the case of actuator jamming or hard-over, there is no need to recompute normals to all facets. We need only remove from consideration those facets that were generated using corresponding columns of the B matrix, and adjust the required pseudo-control vector (we should subtract "jammed" columns as in (Burken et al., 2001)).

4.5 Numerical examples

To illustrate the proposed approach, let us first consider the following 2D control allocation problem taken from (Durham, 1993):

$$B = \begin{bmatrix} 7.35e-4 & 7.55e-4 & -1.35e-4 \\ 8.56e-5 & 5.13e-4 & -1.37e-3 \end{bmatrix}, \begin{bmatrix} -20 \\ -20 \\ -30 \end{bmatrix} \leq u \leq \begin{bmatrix} 20 \\ 20 \\ 30 \end{bmatrix}, y_{des} = \begin{bmatrix} 0.035 \\ 0 \end{bmatrix} \tag{4.20}$$

The advantage of this example is that we can easily do visualization with the algorithm steps in terms of attainable sets, which is not a very straightforward task when we are dealing with problems of higher dimension.

In this case, the algorithm can utilize a very simple computation of normal vectors. As we know that each normal vector to a facet is perpendicular to one of the B columns, we have

$$d_i^T = [-b_i^{(2)},\ b_i^{(1)}], i = \overline{1,3}. \tag{4.21}$$

Control constraints are given in degrees and the pseudo-control vector is actually a vector of the body-axis rolling and yawing moment coefficients:

$$y = \begin{bmatrix} C_l \\ C_n \end{bmatrix}. \tag{4.22}$$

Since the commanded moment appears to be outside the APS, it was first scaled to

$$y = \begin{bmatrix} 0.0286 \\ 0 \end{bmatrix}, \tag{4.22}$$

which lies at the APS boundary. Then we applied 8 bisection steps with 3 iterations for each one. After 24 iterations the following enclosing control box was obtained:

$$\begin{bmatrix} 19.8438 \\ 19.8438 \\ 8.6719 \end{bmatrix} \leq u \leq \begin{bmatrix} 20 \\ 20 \\ 8.9063 \end{bmatrix} \tag{4.24}$$

We can conclude that the final maximal error (the length of the longest facet of this box as in (4.7)) is 0.2344 deg. We found this estimate to be in perfect agreement with the predicted error, which is equal to $60/2^8$ deg.

In Figure 4.7 the moment sets for the left and the right control boxes are shown for the first 8 bisection steps. For each step, we depict by solid lines a box that has been chosen by the algorithm at that iteration, while dashed lines represent the one that has been deleted. The cross inside the circle represents the (scaled) commanded moment vector. One can notice that the union of the two moment sets is always a convex set since it represents the attainable moment set for the union of two adjacent control boxes.

Another example is connected with unstable lateral/directional dynamics of the X-33 vehicle (Burken et al., 2001) at critical conditions during the entry flight, already considered in the Chapter 2, where one can find control surface limits. Instead of moments, we are dealing in this example with angular rates, so that

$$y = \begin{bmatrix} p \\ r \\ q \end{bmatrix}$$

and

$$B = \begin{bmatrix} -0.2137 & 0.2137 & -0.8418 & 0.8418 & 0.0115 & 0.0115 & -0.2612 & 0.2621 \\ 0.0448 & -0.0448 & 0.3639 & -0.3639 & -0.0077 & -0.0077 & 0.0548 & -0.0548 \\ -0.0617 & -0.0617 & -0.5393 & -0.5393 & 0.005 & -0.005 & -0.0754 & 0.0754 \end{bmatrix}.$$

Note that B here is different from B in the Chapter 2 (Burken et al., 2001) since we control only three phase variables.

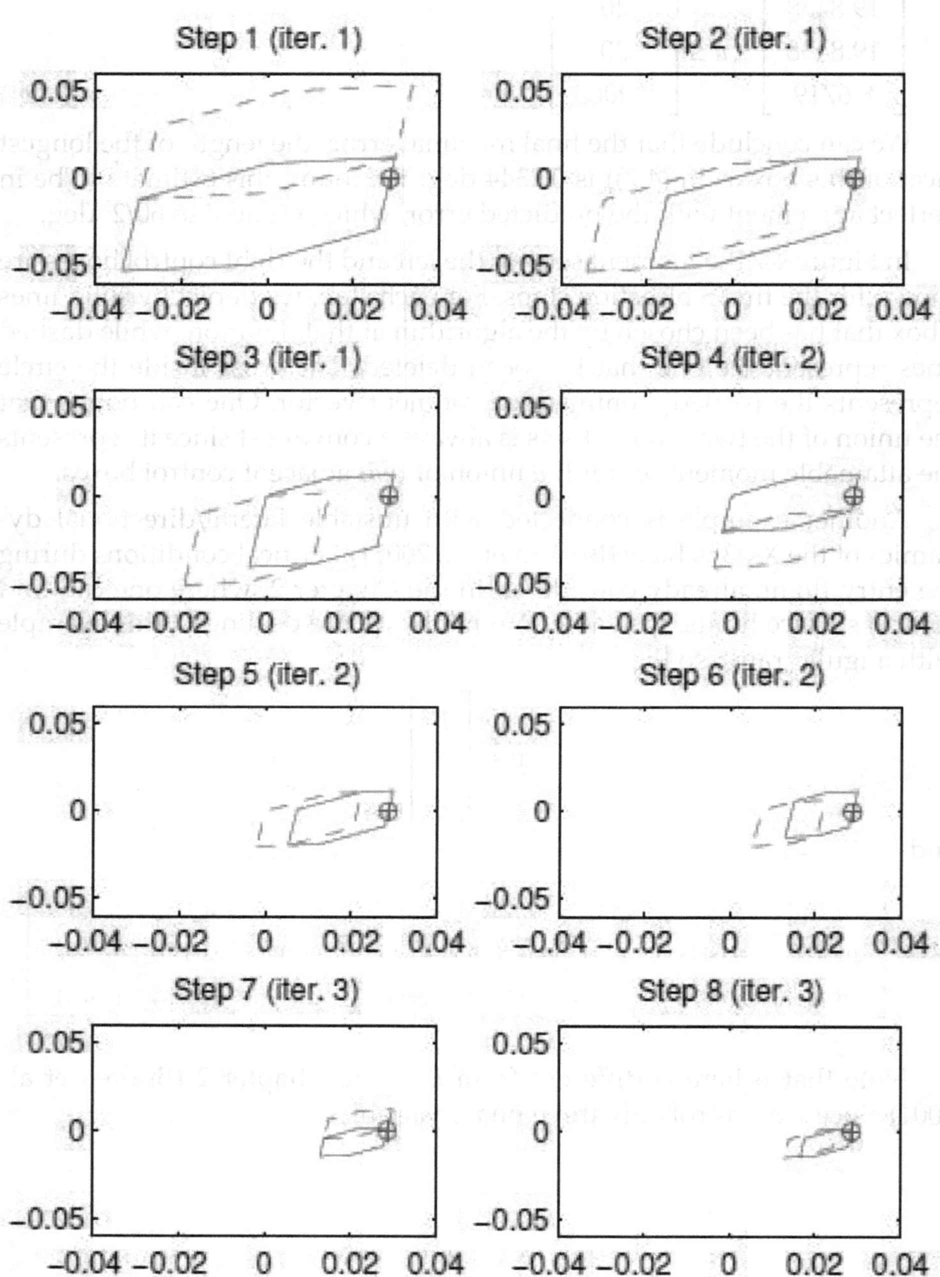

Figure 4.7: Moment sets induced by U_1 (solid) and U_2 (dashed). The horizontal and vertical axes represent the rolling and the yawing moments, respectively. The crossed circle marks y.

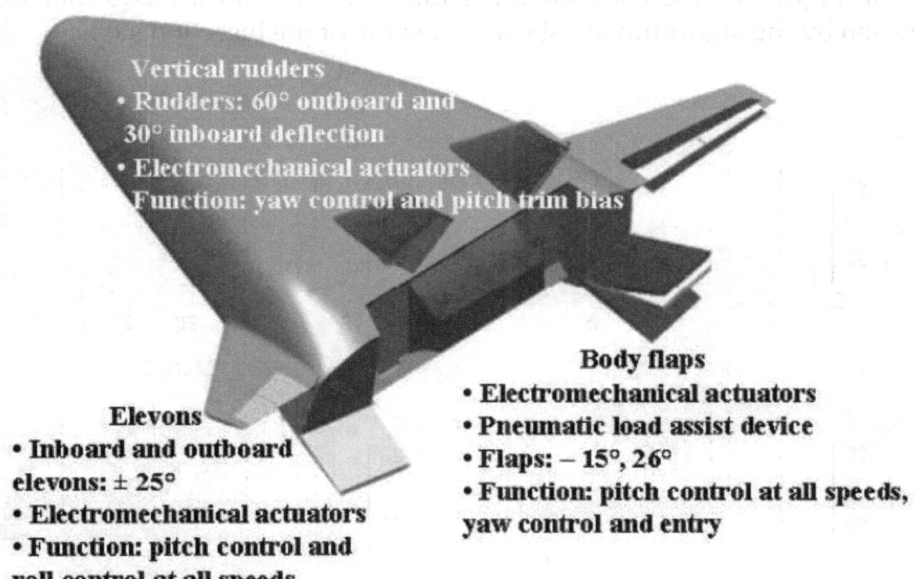

Figure 4.8: The X-33 reusable launch vehicle

Note that for the 3D case every vector perpendicular to a facet of the APS is actually a scaled cross-product of two different columns of the matrix B. So, we can easily compute all possible cross-products $b_i \times b_j$ and be sure that we have caught all directions perpendicular to the AMS facets. This will give us $(m-1)!$ vectors d_k. Some of them are true facet normals, and some may be redundant.

For commanded $p = 10$ deg/sec, $q = r = 0$ the following enclosing control box was obtained after 120 iterations:

$$\begin{bmatrix} -25 \\ 1.1703 \\ 9.5952 \\ 0.11594 \\ -29.991 \\ -29.987 \\ -25 \\ 24.974 \end{bmatrix} \leq u \leq \begin{bmatrix} -24.998 \\ 1.1719 \\ 9.5964 \\ 0.11719 \\ -29.989 \\ -29.985 \\ -24.998 \\ 24.976 \end{bmatrix} \tag{4.25}$$

In Figure 4.9 the corresponding rate sets for control boxes that were chosen by the algorithm are shown for some of the bisection steps.

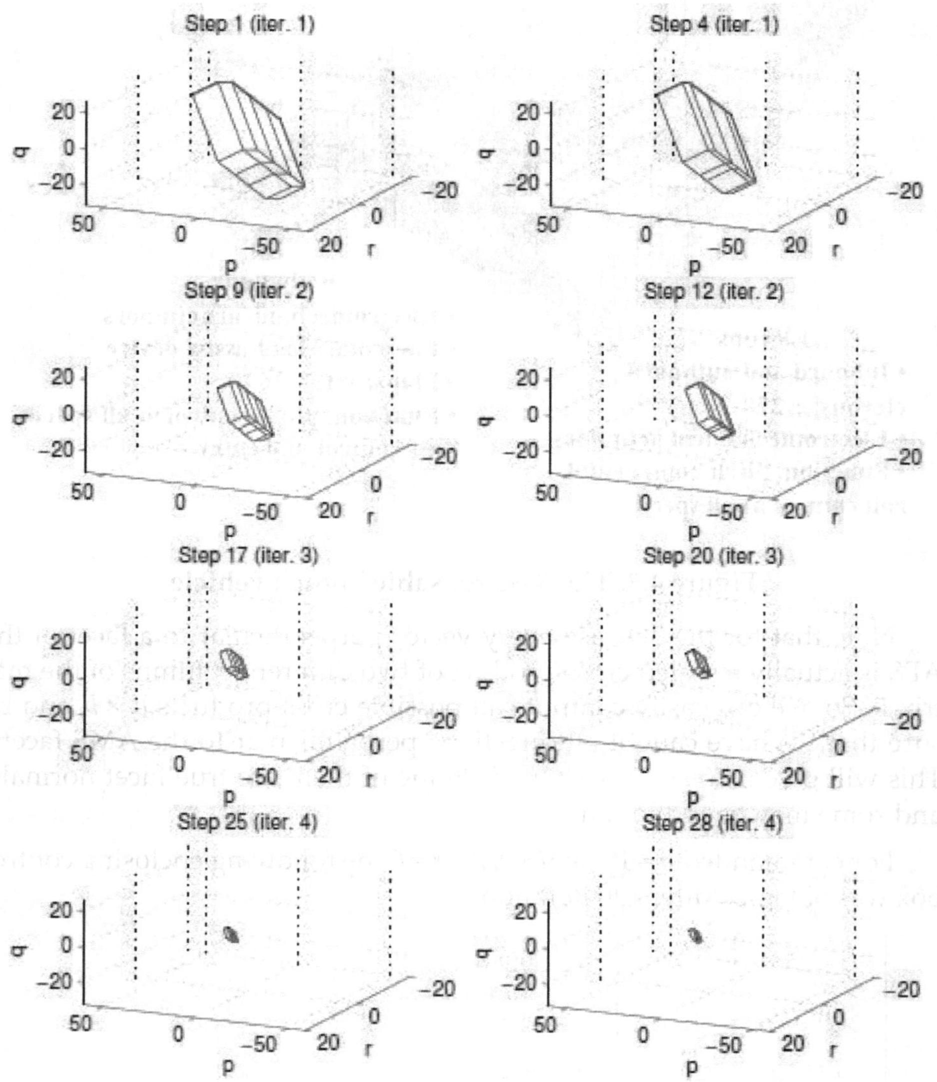

Figure 4.9: Rate sets induced by the control boxes chosen on some steps for 3D example (variables are in degrees per second).

4.6 Conclusion

A novel control allocation algorithm was presented. It has a guarantee of obtaining the solution for any given pseudo-control vector inside the

APS, using normals to the APS facets and the set of control constraints. The computations are performed in a finite number of iterations which are known in advance with required numerical accuracy. These properties allow the algorithm to be considered for implementation in those safety-critical applications where on-line optimization is prohibited while fast reconfiguration in the case of actuator failure is required.

Chapter 5

Conclusions and Plans for Further Work

Controllability of a system is a necessary condition for the successful design of a controller and the starting point in a design is to check whether the system is controllable or not. Hence, tests which check controllability are not only theoretically important but are also useful tools in the control engineer's hands. In this thesis such a tool based on a convex optimization technique is proposed for the computation of the controllable region of an unstable linear system under amplitude and rate control constraints. It can be applied for the post design assessment of different control laws and the specification of the design requirements for the actuator characteristics. Moreover, using computational analysis of the controllable region, for planar systems with both poles exponentially unstable and multiple control inputs, we provide a geometric insight into how to construct a saturated stabilizing linear state feedback so that the domain of attraction of the closed-loop system is maximized.

The significance of the notion of controllability in linear control theory is obvious since many design related questions, such as arbitrary pole placement by state feedback, hinge on the controllability condition. The key to the success of the notion in the linear case is the Kalman controllability criterion, which on one hand describes an open-loop control property (controllability) and which implies a closed-loop property (stabilizability). It should be noted also that the null-time controllability is very closely related to the existence of time-optimal control laws and therefore to the stability optimal control as well. Note, however, that in a nonlinear context, controllability does not imply stabilizability and hence *it does not play the same role for nonlinear systems* from the stabilization point of view.

Therefore, one should not expect the results presented in the first two chapters to be easily extended to the nonlinear case. In the past, a great effort has been devoted to extending the known relation between controllability and stabilizability for linear systems to the nonlinear case (Celikovsky and Nijmeijer, 1997). For nonlinear static-state feedback stabilization, the situation appears to be quite complicated; a well-known example of a controllable system that is not asymptotically stabilizable by means of a smooth feedback was given in (Brockett, 1983). Various relaxations and modifications of the notions of stabilizability and controllability did not help (even a feedback understood in a very general sense is not able to stabilize the Brockett example). A continuous stabilizing feedback fails to exist in general.

It has been shown, however, that every asymptotically controllable nonlinear system can be globally stabilized by means of some discontinuous feedback law (Clarke, Ledyaev, Sontag and Subbotin, 1997; Shim and Teel, 2003). Despite having great theoretical significance, this property does not help in the case of flight control design, especially considering the recent shift towards all-electric aircraft (Schallert, 2007). The maximum control signal rates achieved by the electrical-based actuators can be considerably less than for the previously used hydraulic systems, and this can affect the performance of the closed-loop control system significantly. Note that even for aircraft with a hydraulic actuation system, rate control constraints have been frequently considered as more important and leading to controllability problems such as pilot-induced oscillations (Gilbreath, 2001; Sofrony, Turner, Postlethwaite, Brieger and Leibling, 2006; Brieger, Kerr, Leibling, Postlethwaite, Sofrony and Turner, 2007). There is no way of implementing discontinuous control laws in this situation, and therefore the computation of the controllable region for significantly nonlinear aircraft dynamics makes no sense. The design of any control law that is based on the controllable region computation seems also impossible.

Despite that, the general ideology of this thesis is still applicable in the nonlinear case, if one considers it as set-theoretic approach by which one can either estimate or enlarge some regions in the system state-space and/or parameter space. These regions can be somehow related to the performance of the closed-loop system.

In the third part of the thesis, this ideology has been applied to the computation of the attainable pseudo-control sets and the related maximization of moments and forces available for an aircraft control in the linear case. Since the result is based on the idea of interval bisection, one should expect that the interval analysis, which in recent years has been applied to a number of engineering problems (Jaulin et al., 2001), can help to extend the results for the general nonlinear case.

Recently, more set-based performance criteria have appeared in the literature, for example attainable equilibrium states sets (Goman, Khramtsovsky and Kolesnikov, 2007) or regions of the Lyapunov function existence in the parameter space for robustness analysis (Juliana, Chu and Mulder, 2007). Generally, one should expect such criteria as being formulated in terms of nonlinear equations and inequalities. The answer to the posed problem can be achieved by solving the inequalities via *quantifier elimination* (Jirstrand, 1997). In the linear case, quantifier elimination can be performed via the Fourier-Motzkin variable elimination algorithm, described in Chapter 2 (quantifier "exists"), and Minkowski subtraction (quantifier "for all"). These methods have been used for the computation of controllable sets for discrete-time linear systems with and without external disturbances (Keerthi and Gilbert, 1987; Mayne and Schroeder, 1997).

In the nonlinear case, the elimination process was applied via symbolic computations using the software package QUEPCAD to derive the set of stationary orientations (also called the attainable equilibrium set in (Goman et al., 2007)) for the F-16 aircraft model (Glad and Jirstrand, 1996). Recently, two new methods (Ratschan, 2006; Wittenberg, 2004) and associated software packages (RSOLVER and CLIP) that perform quantifier elimination in nonlinear inequalities numerically via interval analysis have appeared. The problems solvable by these methods include estimation of the region of attraction (Burchardt and Ratschan, 2007) and hybrid systems modelling (Hickey and Wittenberg, 2004).

The author therefore believes that the progress in the further application of the approach used in this thesis is closely connected with the formulation of set-based performance criteria in the form of nonlinear inequalities and solving them by means of quantifier elimination. This includes the development of new methods for nonlinear variable elimination, which could be based on their linear counterparts and the local linearization of the constraints.

Bibliography

Applebaum, E. and Ben-Asher, J. (2007), 'Control of an aeroelastic system with actuator saturation', *Journal of Guidance, Control, and Dynamics* 30(2), 548–556.

Avanzini, G. and Galeani, S. (2005), 'Robust antiwindup for manual flight control of an unstable aircraft', *Journal of Guidance, Control, and Dynamics* 28(6), 1275–1282.

Barbu, C., Galeani, S., Teel, A. and Zaccarian, L. (2005), 'Non-linear anti-windup for manual flight control', *International Journal of Control* 78(14), 1111–1129.

Blanchini, F. (1995), 'Non-quadratic Lyapunov function for robust control', *Automatica* 31, 451–461.

Blanchini, F. (1999), 'Set invariance in control', *Automatica* 35, 1747–1767.

Blanchini, F. and Miani, S. (1996), 'Constrained stabilization of continuous-time linear systems', *Systems and Control Letters* 28, 95–102.

Blanchini, F. and Miani, S. (2007), *Set-theoretic methods in control,* Birkh¨auser, Boston.

Block, J. and Strganac, T. (1998), 'Applied active control for a nonlinear aeroelastic structure', *Journal of Guidance, Control, and Dynamics* 21(6), 838–845.

Bodson, M. (2002), 'Evaluation of optimization methods for control allocation', *Journal of Guidance, Control, and Dynamics* 25(4), 703–711.

Boyd, S., Ghaoui, L., Feron, E. and Balakrishnan, V. (1994), *Linear Matrix Inequalities in System and Control Theory*, SIAM, Philadelphia.

Brieger, O., Kerr, M., Leibling, D., Postlethwaite, I., Sofrony, J. and Turner, M. (2007), Anti-windup compensation of rate saturation in an experimental aircraft, *in* 'Proceedings of the American Control Conference', New York, USA, pp. 924–929.

Brockett, R. (1983), Asymptotic stability and feedback stabilization, *in* R. Brockett, R. Milman and H. Sussmann, eds, 'Differential Geometric Control Theory', Birkhauser, Boston.

Buffington, J. and Enns, D. (1996), 'Lyapunov stability analysis of daisy-chain control allocation', *Journal of Guidance, Control, and Dynamics* 19(6), 1226–1230.

Burchardt, H. and Ratschan, S. (2007), Estimating the region of attraction of ordinary differential equations by quantified constraint solving, *in* 'Proceedings of the 3rd WSEAS International Conference on DYNAMICAL SYSTEMS and CONTROL (CONTROL'07)', WSEAS Press, pp. 241–246.

Burken, J., Lu, P., Wu, Z. and Bahm, C. (2001), 'Two reconfigurable flight control design methods: robust servomechanism and control allocation', *Journal of Guidance, Control, and Dynamics* 24(3), 482–493.

Cameron, D. and Princen, N. (2000), Control allocation challenges and requirements for the blended wing body, *in* 'AIAA Guidance, Navigation and Control Conference Proceedings', Denver, Colorado. AIAA Paper 2000-4539.

Cao, Y., Lin, Z. and Hu, T. (2002), 'Stability analysis of linear time-delay systems subject to input saturation', *IEEE Transactions on Circuits and Systems - I: Fundamental Theory and Applications* 49(2), 233–240.

Cao, Y., Lin, Z. and Ward, D. (2002), 'An antiwindup approach to enlarging domain of attraction for linear systems subject to actuator saturation', *IEEE Transactions on Automatic Control* 47(1), 140–145.

Cao, Y., Lin, Z. and Ward, D. (2004), 'Anti-windup design of output tracking systems subject to actuator saturation and constant disturbances', *Automatica* 40, 1221–1228.

Castelan, E., da Silva Jr., J. G. and Cury, J. (1996), 'A reduced-order framework applied to linear systems with constrained controls', *IEEE Transactions on Automatic Control* 41, 249–255.

Celikovsky, S. and Nijmeijer, H. (1997), 'On the relation between local controllability and stabilizability for a class of nonlinear systems', *IEEE Transactions on Automatic Control* 42(1), 90–94.

Chandru, V. (1993), 'Variable elimination in linear constraints', *Comput. J.* 36, 463–472.

Clarke, F., Ledyaev, Y., Sontag, E. and Subbotin, A. (1997), 'Asymptotic controllability implies feedback stabilization', *IEEE Transactions on Automatic Control* 42(10), 1394– 1407.

da Silva, J. G. and Tarbouriech, S. (1999), 'Polyhedral regions of local stability for linear discrete-time systems with saturating controls', *IEEE Transactions on Automatic Control* 44(11), 2081–2085.

da Silva, J. G. and Tarbouriech, S. (2005), 'Anti-windup design with guaranteed regions of stability: an lmi approach', *IEEE Transactions on Automatic Control* 50(1), 106–111.

da Silva, J. G. and Tarbouriech, S. (2006), 'Anti-windup design with guaranteed regions of stability for discrete-time linear systems', *Systems and Control Letters* 55, 184–192.

Dantzig, G. (1966), *Linear programming and extensions*, Princeton University Press, Princeton.

Demenkov, M. (2005), Reconfigurable linear control allocation via generalized bisection, *in* 'AIAA Guidance, Navigation and Control Conference Proceedings', San Francisco, California. AIAA Paper 2005-6341.

Demenkov, M. (2006), Stability-optimal control for planar unstable systems, *in* 'Proceedings of the UKACC International Control Conference', Glasgow, UK.

Demenkov, M. (2007), Interval bisection method for control allocation, *in* 'Proceedings of the 17th IFAC Symposium on Automatic Control in Aerospace', Toulouse, France.

Doman, D. and Oppenheimer, M. (2002), Improving control allocation accuracy for nonlinear aircraft dynamics, *in* 'AIAA Guidance, Navigation and Control Conference Proceedings', Monterey, California. AIAA Paper 2002-4667.

Duffin, R. (1974), 'On fourier's analysis of linear inequality systems', *Math. Programming Study* 1, 71–95.

Durham, W. (1993), 'Constrained control allocation', *Journal of Guidance, Control, and Dynamics* 16(4), 717–725.

Durham, W. (1994), 'Constrained control allocation: three-moment problem', *Journal of Guidance, Control, and Dynamics* 17(2), 330–336.

Filimonov, A. and Filimonov, N. (1995), The synthesis and optimization of regulation systems by means of the piecewise linear functions of Lyapunov, *in* 'Computer Systems and Research Automation: Proceedings of the 9th SAER Conference and DECUS NUG Seminar', Sofia.

Filimonov, A. and Filimonov, N. (1996), 'Nonsmooth analysis and synthesis of regulation systems via the Lyapunov's direct method, part 2: synthesis and optimization of regulation systems', *Proceedings of the Higher Education Institutions. Ser. Instrument-making* 39(4), 8–23. (in Russian).

Formalsky, A. (1968), 'Controllability domain of systems having limited control resources', *Automation and Remote Control* 29(3), 375–382.

Formalsky, A. (1974), *Controllability and stability of systems with control constraints*, Nauka, Moscow. (in Russian).

Frampton, K. and Clark, R. (2000), 'Experiments on control of limit-cycle oscillations in a typical section', *Journal of Guidance, Control, and Dynamics* 23(5), 956–960.

Friedmann, P. (1999), 'Renaissance of aeroelasticity and its future', *Journal of Aircraft* 36(1), 105–121.

Galeani, S., Teel, A. and Zaccarian, L. (2007), 'Constructive nonlinear anti-windup design for exponentially unstable linear plants', *Systems and Control Letters* 56(5), 357–365.

Gaulocher, S., Roos, C. and Cumer, C. (2007), 'Aircraft load alleviation during maneuvers using optimal control surface combinations', *Journal of Guidance, Control, and Dynamics* 30(2), 591–600.

Gilbreath, G. (2001), Prediction of pilot-induced oscillations due to actuator rate limiting using the open-loop onset point criterion, Master's thesis, Air Force Institute Of Technology.

Glad, T. (1995), Stabilizable regions for unstable systems with rate and amplitude bounds on the control, *in* 'Proceedings of the IFAC Symposium on Nonlinear Control Systems Design', Tahoe City, CA, USA, pp. 489–492.

Glad, T. (1996), Stabilizability under actuator constraints: an application to aircraft control, *in* 'Proceedings of the 12-th International Symposium on the Mathematical Theory of Networks and Systems', St Louis, Missouri.

Glad, T. and Jirstrand, M. (1996), Computational questions of equilibrium calculation with application to nonlinear aircraft dynamics, *in* 'Proceedings of the 12-th International Symposium on the Mathematical Theory of Networks and Systems', St Louis, Missouri.

Goebel, R. (2005), 'Stabilizing a linear system with saturation through optimal control', *IEEE Transactions on Automatic Control* 50(5), 650–655.

Goebel, R. and Subbotin, M. (2007), 'Continuous time constrained linear quadratic regulator – convex duality approach', *IEEE Transactions on Automatic Control* 52(5), 886– 892.

Golub, G. and Loan, C. V. (1986), *Matrix computations*, North Oxford Academic publ., London.

Goman, M. and Demenkov, M. (2002), Controllability region analysis for unstable aircraft dynamics, *in* 'AIAA Guidance, Navigation and Control Conference Proceedings', Monterey, USA. AIAA Paper 2002-4749.

Goman, M. and Demenkov, M. (2004*a*), 'Computation of controllability regions for unstable aircraft dynamics', *AIAA Journal of Guidance, Control and Dynamics* 27, 647–656.

Goman, M. and Demenkov, M. (2004*b*), Stabilization of unstable aircraft dynamics under control constraints, *in* S. Sivasundaram, ed., 'Advances in Dynamics and Control', CRC Press, Boca Raton, Florida.

Goman, M., Fedulova, E. and Khramtsovsky, A. (1996), Maximum stability region design for unstable aircraft with control constraints, *in* 'AIAA Guidance, Navigation and Control Conference Proceedings', San Diego, California. AIAA Paper 96-3910.

Goman, M., Khramtsovsky, A. and Kolesnikov, E. (2007), Investigation of the ADMIRE manoeuvring capabilities using qualitative methods, *in* D. Bates and M. Hagstrom, eds, 'Nonlinear Analysis and Synthesis Techniques for Aircraft Control', Lecture Notes in Control and Information Sciences, Springer, Berlin.

Grishanin, U., Lebedev, G., Lipatov, A. and Stepanjantz, G. (1999), *The optimal dynamical systems theory*, MAI, Moscow. (in Russian).

Gutman, P. and Cwikel, M. (1987), 'An algorithm to find maximal state constraint sets for discrete-time linear dynamical systems with bounded controls and states', *IEEE Transactions on Automatic Control* AC-32(3), 251–254.

Hanson, G. and Stengel, R. (1984), 'Effects of displacement and rate saturation on the control of statically unstable aircraft', *Journal of Guidance, Control, and Dynamics* 7(2), 197–205.

Hartmann, G., Barrett, M. and Greene, C. (1979), Control design for an unstable vehicle, Contract report, NASA Dryden Flight Research Center. NAS 4-2578.

Henrion, D. and Tarbouriech, S. (1999), 'Lmi relaxations for robust stability of linear systems with saturating controls', *Automatica* 35(9), 1599–1604.

Henrion, D., Tarbouriech, S. and Garcia, G. (1999), 'Output feedback robust stabilization of uncertain linear systems with saturating controls: an lmi approach', *IEEE Transactions on Automatic Control* 44(11), 2230–2237.

Henrion, D., Tarbouriech, S. and Kuˇcera, V. (2001), 'Control of linear systems subject to input constraints: a polynomial approach', *Automatica* 37(4), 597–604.

Hickey, T. and Wittenberg, D. (2004), Rigorous modeling of hybrid systems using interval arithmetic constraints, *in* R.Alur and G. Pappas, eds, 'Hybrid Systems: Computation and Control (HSCC 2004)', Vol. 2993 of *Lecture Notes in Computer Science*, Springer Verlag, pp. 402–416.

Hu, T., Goebel, R., Teel, A. and Lin, Z. (2005), 'Conjugate Lyapunov functions for saturated linear systems', *Automatica* 41(11), 1949–1956.

Hu, T. and Lin, Z. (2000), 'On enlarging the basin of attraction for linear systems under saturated linear feedback', *Systems and Control Letters* 40, 59–69.

Hu, T. and Lin, Z. (2001*a*), 'A complete stability analysis of planar discrete-time linear systems under saturation', *IEEE Transactions on Circuits and Systems - I: Fundamental Theory and Applications* 48(6), 710–725.

Hu, T. and Lin, Z. (2001*b*), *Control systems with actuator saturation: analysis and design*, Birkh¨auser, Boston.

Hu, T. and Lin, Z. (2001*c*), 'Practical stabilization of exponentially unstable linear systems subject to actuator saturation nonlinearity and disturbance', *International Journal of Robust and Nonlinear Control* 11, 555–588.

Hu, T. and Lin, Z. (2002*a*), 'Exact characterization of invariant ellipsoid for single input linear systems subject to actuator saturation', *IEEE Transactions on Automatic Control* 47(1), 164–169.

Hu, T. and Lin, Z. (2002*b*), 'On semi-global stabilizability of anti-stable systems by saturated linear feedback', *IEEE Transactions on Automatic Control* 47(7), 1193–1198.

Hu, T. and Lin, Z. (2003), 'Composite quadratic Lyapunov functions for constrained control systems', *IEEE Transactions on Automatic Control* 48(3), 440–450.

Hu, T., Lin, Z. and Chen, B. (2002*a*), 'Analysis and design for discrete-time linear systems subject to actuator saturation', *Systems and Control Letters* 45(1), 97–112.

Hu, T., Lin, Z. and Chen, B. (2002*b*), 'An analysis and design method for linear systems subject to actuator saturation and disturbance', *Automatica* 38, 351–359.

Hu, T., Lin, Z. and Qiu, L. (2001), 'Stabilization of exponentially unstable linear systems with saturating actuators', *IEEE Transactions on Automatic Control* 46, 973–979.

Hu, T., Lin, Z. and Qiu, L. (2002), 'An explicit description of the null controllable regions of linear systems with saturating actuators', *Systems and Control Letters* 47(1), 65–78.

Hu, T., Lin, Z. and Shamash, Y. (2001), 'Semi-global stabilization with guaranteed regional performance of linear systems subject to actuator saturation', *Systems and Control Letters* 43, 203–210.

Hu, T., Miller, D. and Qiu, L. (2002), 'Null controllable region of LTI discrete-time systems with input saturation', *Automatica* 38(11), 2009–2013.

Jaulin, L., Kieffer, M., Didrit, O. and Walter, E. (2001), *Applied Interval Analysis*, Springer-Verlag, London.

Jirstrand, M. (1997), 'Nonlinear control system design by quantifier elimination', *Journal of Symbolic Computation* 24(2), 137–152.

Johansen, T., Fossen, T. and Tondel, P. (2005), 'Efficient optimal constrained control allocation via multiparametric programming', *Journal of Guidance, Control, and Dynamics* 28(3), 506–515.

Julian, P., Guivant, J. and Desages, A. (1999), 'A parametrization of piecewise linear Lyapunov functions via linear programming', *International Journal of Control* 72(7/8), 702–715.

Juliana, S., Chu, Q. and Mulder, J. (2007), Nonlinear re-entry flight control system robustness evaluation using interval analysis, *in* 'Proceedings of the 17th IFAC Symposium on Automatic Control in Aerospace', Toulouse, France.

Kamenetskiy, V. (1995), 'A method for construction of stability regions by Lyapunov functions', *Systems and Control Letters* 26, 147–151.

Kamenetskiy, V. (1996), Construction of a constrained stabilizing feedback by Lyapunov functions, *in* 'Proceedings of the 13th IFAC World Congress', San Francisco, USA, pp. 139–144. (2b-04 6).

Keerthi, S. and Gilbert, E. (1987),'Computation of minimum-time feedback control laws for discrete-time systems with state-control constraints', *IEEE Transactions on Automatic Control* AC-32(5), 432–435.

Ko, J., Strganac, T. and Kurdila, A. (1998), 'Stability and control of a structurally nonlinear aeroelastic system', *Journal of Guidance, Control, and Dynamics* 21(5), 718–725.

Kohler, D. (1967), Projections of convex polyhedral sets, Operations research centre report, University of California, Berkeley. ORC 67-29.

Lasserre, J. (1993), 'Reachable, controllable sets and stabilizing control of constrained linear systems', *Automatica* 29(2), 531–536.

Lee, A. and Hedrick, J. (1995), 'Some new results on closed-loop stability in the presence of control saturation', *International Journal of Control* pp. 619–631.

Lin, Z. and Hu, T. (2001), 'Semi-global stabilization of linear systems subject to output saturation', *Systems and Control Letters* 43, 211–217.

Ma, C. (1991), 'Unstabilizability of linear unstable systems with input limits', *ASME Journal of dynamic systems, measurement, and control* 113, 742–744.

Maciejowski, J. (2002), *Predictive Control with Constraints*, Prentice Hall, London. MathWorks (2001*a*), *Optimization Toolbox User's Guide*.

MathWorks (2001*b*), *Robust Control Toolbox for use with MATLAB*.

Mayne, D. and Schroeder, W. (1997), 'Robust time-optimal control of constrained linear systems', *Automatica* 33(12), 2103–2118.

McMullen, P. and Shepard, G. (1971), *Convex polytopes and the upper bound conjecture*, Cambridge University Press, Cambridge.

Mukhopadhyay, V. (2000), 'Transonic flutter suppression control law design and wind-tunnel test results', *Journal of Guidance, Control, and Dynamics* 23(5), 930–937.

Mukhopadhyay, V. (2003), 'Historical perspective on analysis and control of aeroelastic responses', *Journal of Guidance, Control, and Dynamics* 26(5), 673–684.

Ngo, A., Reigelsperger, W., Banda, S. and Bessolo, J. (1996), Multivariable control law design of a tailless airplane, *in* 'AIAA Guidance, Navigation and Control Conference Proceedings', San Diego, CA. AIAA Paper 96-3866.

Pare, T., Hindi, H., How, J. and Boyd, S. (1998), Synthesizing stability regions for systems with saturating actuators, *in* 'Proceedings of the 37th IEEE Conference on Decision & Control', pp. 1981–1982.

Peterfreund, N. and Baram, Y. (1998), 'Convergence analysis of nonlinear dynamical systems by nested Lyapunov functions', *IEEE Transactions on Automatic Control* 43(8), 1179–1184.

Petersen, J. and Bodson, M. (2000), Control allocation for systems with coplanar controls, *in* 'AIAA Guidance, Navigation and Control Conference Proceedings'. AIAA Paper 2000-4540.

Petersen, J. and Bodson, M. (2002), 'Fast implementation of direct allocation with extension to coplanar controls', *Journal of Guidance, Control, and Dynamics* 25(3), 464–473.

Pontryagin, L., Boltyanskii, V., Gamkrelidze, R. and Mishchenko, E. (1962), *The mathematical theory of optimal processes*, John Wiley & Sons, New York.

Ratschan, S. (2006), 'Efficient solving of quantified inequality constraints over the real numbers', *ACM Transactions on Computational Logic* 7(4), 723–748.

Rossiter, J., Kouvaritakis, B. and Rice, M. (1998), 'A numerically robust state-space approach to stable-predictive control strategies', *Automatica* 34(1), 65–73.

Rourke, J. O. (1994), *Computational geometry in C*, Cambridge University Press, Cambridge.

Schallert, C. (2007), Concept for the design of flight control actuation and laws for future all-electric aircraft, *in* 'Proceedings of the 17th IFAC Symposium on Automatic Control in Aerospace', Toulouse, France.

Scibile, L. (1997), Non-linear control of the plasma vertical position in a tokamak, PhD thesis, Oxford University.

Scibile, L. and Kouvaritakis, B. (2000), 'Stability region for a class of open-loop unstable linear systems: theory and application', *Automatica* 36(1), 37–44.

Scott, R. and Pado, L. (2000), 'Active control of wind tunnel model aeroelastic response using neural networks', *Journal of Guidance, Control, and Dynamics* 23(6), 1100–1108.

Shim, H. and Teel, A. (2003), 'Asymptotic controllability and observability imply semiglobal practical asymptotic stabilizability by sampled-data output feedback', *Automatica* 39, 441–454.

Shrivastava, P. and Stengel, R. (1989), 'Stability boundaries for aircraft with unstable lateral-directional dynamics and control saturation', *Journal of Guidance, Control, and Dynamics* 12(1), 62–70.

Sofrony, J., Turner, M., Postlethwaite, I., Brieger, O. and Leibling, D. (2006), Anti-windup synthesis for pio avoidance in an experimental aircraft, *in* 'Proceedings of the 45th IEEE Conference on Decision and Control', San Diego, USA.

Stepanjantz, G. (1985), *Theory of dynamical systems*, Mashinostroenie, Moscow. (in Russian).

Tarbouriech, S., da Silva, J. G. and Garcia, G. (2003), 'Delay-dependent anti-windup loops for enlarging the stability region of time-delay systems with saturating inputs', *ASME Journal of Dynamic Systems, Measurement and Control* 125(2), 265–267.

Tarbouriech, S., Queinnec, I. and Garcia, G. (2006), 'Stability region enlargement through anti-windup strategy for linear systems with dynamics restricted actuator', *International Journal of Systems Science* 37(2), 79–90.

Turner, M. and Postlethwaite, I. (2001), 'Guaranteed stability regions of linear systems with actuator saturation using the low-and-high gain technique', *International Journal of Control* 74(14), 1425–1434.

Waszak, M. (1998), Modeling the benchmark active control technology wind-tuneel model for active control design applications, Technical report, NASA. TP-1998-206270.

Waszak, M. (2001), 'Robust multivariable flutter suppression for the benchmark active control technology wind tunnel model', *Journal of Guidance, Control, and Dynamics* 24(1), 147–153.

Wittenberg, D. (2004), CLP(F) Modeling of Hybrid Systems, PhD thesis, Brandeis University.

Zhao, Y. and Jayasariya, S. (1995), 'Stabilizability of unstable linear plants under bounded control', *Journal of Dynamical Systems, Measurement and Control* 117, 63–73.

Ziegler, G. (1995), *Lectures on polytopes*, Vol. 152 of *Graduate Texts in Mathematics*, Springer-Verlag, New York.

INDEX